Tulips to Thresholds

To Ray Nickerson
in appreciation of
our friendship

John Sweto

Tulips to Thresholds

Counterpart Careers
of the Author and
Signal Detection Theory

John A. Swets

Peninsula Publishing
Los Altos Hills, California

Peninsula Publishing
26666 Birch Hill Way
Los Altos Hills, CA 94022
United States of America

Telephone: 650-948-2511
Facsimile: 650-948-5004
Email: sales@PeninsulaPublishing.com
Web site: www.PeninsulaPublishing.com

Cover Design: Kristina Verplank
Printed and bound: Lightning Source, La Vergne, TN
Printed in the United States of America

ISBN 978-0-932146-71-7

Library of Congress Control Number 2010922746

Contents

Foreword

This story in the main is a *personal memoir*. I write of my family background and my formative years, and of my training and career in scientific psychology and beyond. A strong parallel thread in this memoir, going beyond the purely personal, is the story of a theory with which I have been closely associated, namely, *signal detection theory*. I tell of the theory's career in psychology and beyond, including its application to a wide range of diagnostic problems, particularly in medicine.

My career and the theory's have run as counterparts to each other for their durations, beginning with my doctoral thesis and extending into the present. The evolutions of the theory and its applications have largely determined the moves I have made and the positions I have held in academe and research organizations. Contributions I made to the theory have helped to give it a wide range of application.

A third dimension of this memoir is the glimpse it supplies of how academic and scientific psychology have fared at some major institutions in the last half century. These are settings in which I have enjoyed working—including the University of Michigan, Massachusetts Institute of Technology (MIT), Bolt Beranek and Newman Inc. (BBN), Harvard Medical School, and the National Academy of Sciences (NAS).

In my personal account, I relate aspects of my life that no one but me was in a position to witness in their continuity: my youth with my parents and close relatives, my youthful adventures and misadventures with childhood cronies, my adult family life with my wife Maxine

("Mickey") and our sons Stephen and Joel, and my professional life with numerous colleagues added along the way.

In telling of my heritage and the nurturing influences on my youth, I hope to indicate *how* I came to travel the adult path I did, and to shed light on *why*. The reader will see how I have deliberately followed the leads of individuals I admired and perhaps may see how I was pointed along the way by genetic predispositions that clicked with circumstances.

My friends and acquaintances in science may read this story to learn facts and get insights into my professional life that they don't have and so fill in some missing pieces. They might skim the chapters on my early life and see if they recognize the man they know, in the boy I describe. My friends who are not psychology professionals may skim later chapters on my life's work, and find mostly material that will be new, and even strange, to them. I have never been very good at describing in a sentence or two what I do professionally, partly because I claim to be a psychologist and what I do doesn't sound like psychology.

Signal Detection Theory (SDT) comes with a break-through analytical technique called the *Receiver Operating Characteristic (ROC)*. The ROC gives a more reliable and valid measure of detection accuracy—and discrimination, decision, and diagnostic accuracy—than otherwise available and shows how to adjust the decision threshold to achieve the best balance between true-positive and false-positive decisions.

Probably the largest audience for this book consists of those investigators who have come to use the ROC as a disembodied statistical technique. They may now find it attractive to learn of the history and scientific grounding of the concepts that support the ROC through an insider's memoir.

Tulips to Thresholds

1 Through the Tulips

I arrived in the summer of 1928 at Butterworth Hospital in Grand Rapids, Michigan—long, thin, and early enough that the doctor wondered if I would live. My parents had come 'home' for the occasion from the town of Holly in the central part of the state where Dad was teaching high-school history and coaching baseball and basketball. After a year we moved to Holland, Michigan—known for its Tulip Festival—where Dad had been appointed principal of the Christian High School. We lived in Holland thirteen years; this first chapter is how I remember those years.

But first, what sort of lad had the experiences I'm about to recount? Foremost, I think, my mother gave me her determination and my dad gave me his sense of humor. I mean, I could always really focus and I have had a tendency to be amused when I should be grave. How much of this was nature and how much was nurture is an open question, but there is a shyness gene, and both parents contributed to mine. For the three of us, this trait was more likely to surface in intimate settings than in front of larger groups. Anyhow, I was a sensitive youngster, and gangling to boot, though calm, if only by determination.

Roots

Mother was Sara—she preferred Sally—Henrietta Heyns. Dad was John

A., no middle name but the "A" was from his father Arie. I am John Arthur, so not a "junior." My sister Mary Louise joined our family when she was three and I was six.

Grandparents Arie and Kate Swets moved to Grand Rapids from a farm in South Holland, Illinois, so that their ten children could attend the Christian schools there, including Calvin College. It was quite a financial risk for my grandparents to part with that much free farm labor. Grandfather apparently meant to recoup by taking up house construction, a business in which at least the sons could work. My dad specialized in lathing. Grandfather built dozens of houses in Grand Rapids and had them returned to him during the Great Depression, when they were worth less than he was invested in them (and no bailout was available to him). So he was free to build a house for my family in Holland.

Grandparents William and Hendrika Heyns, with nine children, moved to Grand Rapids from Roseland, Illinois, also just south of Chicago, in order for him to take up a professorship at Calvin Seminary.[1] Edna Ferber wrote of the Dutch in Roseland in her novel *So Big*. Her village idiot was "Harm Tien," which happened to be the name of my mother's grandfather. Mother was incensed: how could someone whose daughter married a seminary professor be an idiot?

Emigrating from the Netherlands, Harm Tien and family had landed in Chicago because they slept through a train connection, possibly at Cincinnati, that would have taken them to western Michigan. As Chicago expanded to the south, Tien would sell his farm for house lots and move on to the next farmland to repeat this maneuver. The locals said that he "slept his way to riches." Hearsay has it that he lost his fortune in sugar-beet speculation.

Grandfather Heyns emigrated from the Netherlands with his parents at age twenty-five, after some theological education and military service. I remember seeing him once—he died when I was five—in his large study. He logged many hours on his typewriter there, publishing about 150 articles and a handful of books, notably a *Manual of Reformed Doctrine*.[2]

---

1. South Holland and Roseland might be thought of as "twin towns;" the former was called "Low Prairie" and the latter, "High Prairie."

2. I received a telephone call a few months ago from a seminary student at Calvin College who is writing a thesis on William Heyns.

A New House

We first rented a house in Holland for two years, next to the Vanderveens. I remember well the young neighbor girls Ruthie and Frieda who doted on me. Their goldfish fascinated me. Once they dropped me on my head on a cement sidewalk while swinging me in their crossed arms and clasped wrists; I can still feel the bump and bald spot and could walk to the location on the sidewalk now.

My grandfather built a house for us when I was three. I remember that I wandered off once while supposedly under his care at the building site. After hours of family consternation, I was returned by the police, who had preserved my equanimity with candy treats.

Neighbor Mina "Tiny" Ash was my compadre for the next several years in the new house. She told me that our parents had come on foot together from a far-away place and that her dad had carried both her and me when it became necessary to jump across a large body of water. And she told me not to tell anyone. I was spooked. One time my mother came upon us in a closet with illumination provided by headlights of a toy truck; I think we were having an informational exchange.

Tiny and I walked together to our first day in kindergarten with her sister Janie. I was familiar with Miss Sue Jacobusse's classroom, having visited it several times when my mother was called at the last minute to substitute for a teacher. Mom retrieved a little wooden chair when the kindergarten was refurbished and it is here in my study.

Our Church

Our house was two short blocks from our church. This proximity was handy in the absence of a car, permitting us to attend the hour-and-a-half morning service, then Sunday school, boys' club in the afternoon, and the church service in the evening.[3] Dad fried pork chops for the noon meal. I won a pencil at the boys' club for being first to realize "Who was the father of the sons of Zebedee?" The minister was so austere that he couldn't cope with the kids when they raised havoc during Wednesday's catechism class. Dad naturally did better leading the Young Men's Group on Wednesday.

---

3. Our congregation had recently given up the Dutch-language service in the afternoon.

The Great Depression

That Sunday meal, which included boiled potatoes and canned corn, was quite a treat. Sometimes a Depression meal would be Karo syrup on red kidney beans. I recall once walking to Schadalee's grocery store to pick up our dinner—a can of stewed tomatoes for dipping white bread. At a friend's house, I came to realize that a plate of home-grown yellow beans was the complete meal.

The Depression lagged on and it was 1935 before we could afford a car. (It was the only black Ford with red wheels in town, so Dad could not hide his whereabouts.) The school for awhile paid him five dollars every two weeks (one dollar of which went to my mother's brother Nick, out of work in Muskegon). Because the students' parents were generally behind in tuition payments, Dad would receive some salary in kind, for example, a ton of coal. One Christmas eve he successfully approached the owner of Vogelsang's Hardware to contribute some toys for me.

I was the youngest member of our street gang, which may have been shaped by the hard times. I went along on an escapade to pilfer some objects from an unattended service garage of a Packard automobile agency. In a weak moment I revealed all to my parents who organized a return of the loot along with apologies. I think I lost my 'street cred' that day.

My first bicycle was second-hand—rebuilt, hand-painted, and very spare. When I could choose a new bike, I loaded it up with accessories so it looked more like a Harley than a Schwinn. The trouble was, it was so heavy that I couldn't pump it more than a block.

The Culture

One day I went home sobbing because Jimmy knocked me down while I was on roller skates. As with all fathers and sons, my dad told me to go back and clean his clock, which I managed to do. I mention that Jimmy was the only Roman Catholic boy I knew and that I had no idea what that term meant, in order to touch on Holland's cultural uniformity. The town of 15,000 had one Roman Catholic church, about ten Reformed churches, and about fifteen Christian Reformed churches. Even now, I don't know the doctrinal difference between the two Dutch Reformed denominations, but I remember that ours, Christian Reformed, was the purer. Indeed, when my dad's youngest brother Bill became a

Reformed church pastor, he was thought to be the black sheep of the family.[4]

There were a few other church parishes in Holland—adding up near-ly to one for each of the town's thirty-two streets. These were small and maybe nondenominational. A couple of them were in basements long awaiting a first floor, but one of them was a handsome brick structure. I visited some of them a few times; they were less severe than my church and had much better hymns.

I knew a native American family, but no African or Asian Americans. I suppose there were immigrant laborers out in the black-loamed coun-tryside. The town's "diversity," it seemed to me, came from its two "crazy" men: Jan Ryal, jobless and living in a refurbished chicken coop supplied by the Bouma family, roamed the town telling dirty, albeit clever, jokes to young boys; Sam Wise, who lived in a shack he cobbled together from discarded materials, was spotted around town but, except for announcing that he would vote for the Socialist Norman Thomas, kept his own counsel.[5]

Relatives and Best Friends

Our family was close to the families of my mother's brother Garrett Heyns and my dad's brother Seymour ("Cy") Swets. Garrett held a Ph.D. in history from the University of Michigan and was the superin-tendent of the Holland Christian Schools who hired my dad as princi-pal of the high school. I never heard one whisper of the nepotism in that working arrangement. It must have gone over easy because when Gar-rett moved on eight years later, Dad succeeded him as superintendent. The two men had a strong respect for one another; further, I would say that my dad admired Garrett and he enjoyed my dad.

Uncle Cy was a professor of music at Calvin College for fifty years, like Dad holding an M.A. degree from the University of Michigan. Cy and Dad were pals. Cousin Jack was a year and a half older than I and

---

4. Just kidding ... I think.

5. In 2008, however, a huge step was taken to promote diversity; I almost can't believe it: Holland Christian High hired an African-American football coach, from South Flori-da's hotbed of high school football—Pahokie, I think, or Bel Glade. The man has a young family, so apparently the school is prepared to integrate them. They're doing me proud.

tolerated the difference nicely. He and I exchanged a week's visit each summer and my family often visited his at a cottage on Lake Michigan.

My sister and I would visit the Heynses, attracted partly by home-made ice cream and the player piano. I was encouraged by Dad to see cousin Bob, ten years older, as a model and I responded well, following him to the University of Michigan to study psychology. Bob then left me behind, serving as vice president of the University of Michigan and chancellor of the University of California at Berkeley, among other prominent academic and foundation positions.[6]

Politics

I well remember going to the polls with my dad so he could vote for FDR, in 1932, when I was four. My political interests were reinforced at age eight, when I campaigned for my Uncle Garrett's election to the U.S. Congress as a Democrat from the fifth district of Michigan. Uncle Garrett could only be expected to strengthen the ticket in that Republican stronghold, and was appointed warden of the Michigan Reformatory in Ionia when a Democratic governor was installed. The wisdom behind this second seemingly abrupt career change for Garrett was confirmed when he was later elected president of the American Penology Association. He also became director of corrections for Michigan and then, after he retired, director of institutions for Washington state—where, I'm told, both political parties asked him to run for governor.

I stayed at the warden's Ionia residence a few weeks each summer for three to four years; my Aunt Rosa was an elegant lady and we had a bond. My dad was appointed superintendent of the Boys Vocational School—the state "reform school" in Lansing, Michigan—five years later, in my early teens. It's no surprise that my memories of penal institutions are vivid.

Consider a case of reverse politics. My class held elections for class officers for the first time in the seventh grade. At that time, humility was essential to being elected to anything; one had to say he or she didn't want the honor and look convincing. I was elected class president. I was so humble that my parents learned of my election from someone else weeks later.

Class elections could be a bit of a problem for me. Also in the seventh

---

6. By this time, though privately the same informal guy, professionally he was known by his rightful name, "Roger."

grade, we held a mock election for president and governor, raising a hand to vote. For president, the vote was twenty-six to four for the Republican. For governor, it was twenty-nine to one. You guessed it: only my hand in the air. What's worse is that the Republican gubernatorial candidate had made a strong appeal for the Christian vote. A classmate blurted out: 'Why Johnny, aren't you a Christian?'[7]

Prison Life

The times I spent at the Ionia prison, away from my family in summers and with my family on many holidays, centered in the warden's grand residence. Sweeping gardens in front, tennis court/ice rink in back, a couple hundred yards up to a large swimming pool through grounds roamed by deer and providing bob-sled runs, greenhouse off to one side, and so on. A very handsome house had dozens of rooms of all descriptions, several recreational. Family and five houseboys gathered to listen to Joe Louis's fights; I got his autograph when he brought his Brown Bombers softball team to the prison. One holiday evening we rolled up the living-room rugs to enjoy some inmate tap dancers. I went every day to the Michigan State Free Fair for its week of delights. I went inside the prison walls—to the gym or to the baseball field usually. The four clanging gates, one locked before the next was opened, sounded better when one was leaving than when entering. I traveled on a bus with the baseball team to nearby towns. I ran the manual switchboard at times.

I became acquainted with the house boys: eighteen-year-old Red Mc-Callister, whose mother ran the Purple Gang in Detroit; Demetrius Karemesenis, who had stolen food for his children; Pat (his last name escapes me), who made me a hammered copper tray that is in my eyesight now; and with baseball-team catcher Willie Waas, a lifer who violated parole two days after it was granted because he could no longer cope with the "outside." Willie was an outlier; in general, the Ionia inmates were first offenders of an age skewed toward eighteen to twenty-five years, appropriate for "Doc" Heyns and his education-rehabilitation approach.

My dad requested that the prison psychologist give me an I.Q. test, as I turned eleven. After two days of testing, Dr. James Raymond reported

---

7. I'm still a politics junkie—I regularly read about it and watch cable news and punditry.

an I.Q. and mental age from both a Binet scale and the Grace Arthur scale. The numbers were pretty good, but not as high, I'm sure, as those my later, closest professional colleagues would have produced. He wrote: "[John] is probably somewhat more sensitive and 'intuitive' than the casual observer might expect" and "He should probably be encouraged to work with his hands." I received that encouragement, but its effect lasted only partway through one model airplane.

On Christmas day in Ionia in 1949, we convinced my mother and dad to go to the January 1 Rose Bowl game, featuring the University of Michigan. They took the train, arriving just in time, and reached the Michigan ticket manager, who gave them two tickets for their pluck. Michigan won.

Music

Cy Swets was choir director in a Grand Rapids church (La Grave Avenue) and he didn't miss a Sunday in forty years. He was also a member of the denomination's committee to produce its hymnal, along with my grandfather Heyns.

The Garrett Heynses would drive thirty miles to that church from Ionia for the evening service. Cy would occasionally present a program of tenor solos at the prison. The inmates adored him and called him "Seymour, the Songmeister." Their anticipation would start building when he began "Old Man River" and the great hall would erupt when he reached "get a little drunk and LAND ... IN ... JAI ... LLL."

As head of the music department at Calvin, he conducted the "Messiah" oratorio annually, filling the spacious Civic Auditorium. He himself marveled at this appreciation of music at Calvin College, aware that John Calvin was generally thought to be an enemy of music and art. The secondary Christian schools in my time did little to foster an appreciation of the world's music, art, and literature, consistently reflecting an insular culture. I was a senior in college before it occurred to me to elect a literature course (my advisor applauded).

We did have music in the house; our den included a wind-up Victrola phonograph in a console and an upright piano. Dad could play "by ear" and we sat together on the bench, often singing our favorite hymns. I took piano lessons for about four years toward the end of this chapter's thirteen-year span and then for three more. My first teacher had me practice curving my fingers for what seemed like full time and the second had me practice only the piece I would play at that year's recital. My buddies would hear about my recital and tease me unmercifully about my spectacular rendition of "The Juba Dance," or "Nature in a Joyous Mood."

Parent-Teachers Association

Dad took over from Garrett the superintendence of the Holland Christian school system, adding grades kindergarten through eight to his grades nine through twelve responsibility, in 1937, when I was nine and in the fourth grade. I might be excused for wondering how this father-son connection would work out. Dad walked through the kindergarten through sixth-grade classrooms perhaps monthly. I suppose that because all the teachers were female he sometimes convened the boys of a few classes for a chat; one day he told us that we should aim better at the urinals. Another time he came to the playground and suggested we hit our lively new softball away from a classroom building that jutted into the softball diamond; I slammed the next pitch onto a windowsill and he continued walking away, taking my message. But those comments are flip and don't do him justice; he was a brick, as always.

If I thought having Dad as superintendent was problematic, what might I have thought of having Mom as teacher? She taught my sixth-grade class for a semester, as a last-minute substitute. It wasn't bad at all. Most of the guys had had milk and cookies in our kitchen, and she was a superb teacher.

Affecting Behavior

As teacher as well as mother, Mom was so skillful a behavior coach ("disciplinarian" would be the wrong word) that no one noticed, or could figure out why they were behaving themselves. I drew on her ways in raising my boys: the more you want their attention, the softer you speak.

Dad's behavior-modification techniques could be subtle or not, as the spirit moved him. When I was small, he would threaten me with a dif-FIC'-ul-ty, and while I wondered what that would be, my behavior would resume being acceptable. Alternatively, he might give me a boot in the pants, lifting me off the floor with his instep applied to my padded area, with me hitting the floor pointed toward my room, where I understood I should go to think things over. His versatility stood him in good stead when he had 400 "reform school" inmates in his charge. My mother, I should say, was more practical psychologist than good just at affecting behavior; she told me once that my friends wished they were as tall as I was, thus instantly erasing my concern for my being gangling.

A last example of the subtle call for order that was second nature to my favorite teachers: the ruddy, rugged Visser twins had been the scourge of teachers from kindergarten on and then entered the eighth grade taught by Mrs. Fopma, a minister's wife. She co-opted them on the first day by giving Harvey a permanent hall pass so he could collect absentee slips from the other classrooms and giving Delmar some other job in evidence of her trust. The poor boys hung around her room every day after school to see what else they might do for her and gave her the cleanest blackboards in the building. She never had to exercise her main disciplinary weapon, namely, raising one eyebrow. That eyebrow was mainly a "Surely you wouldn't disappoint me"—and a latent "Just watch yourself, Buster."

In grades four to six, the Visser twins were joint second in the playground pecking order. Everyone believed Mel Tubergen could lick each of them so he never had to prove it. Eugene Brink was a distant fourth till I bluffed him and then I was a really distant fourth. I was sure that Dale Artz could thrash me but he was content in sixth place.

Halloween

My street gang would act up on Halloween, almost feeling social approval because there were particular nights in the preceding week to throw specified things on the porches of neighbors we didn't like: three nights before was cabbage night, two nights before was tomato night, and so on. Mr. Ten Cate was our target. Another mean thing was to make a noisemaker of a spool: by cutting notches around the edges, running a nail through the hole, and winding a cord around the spool. Then we would hold the spool against a window with the nail and jerk the cord; the loud rat-a-tat would frighten everyone in the house.

A more benign Halloween occurred after we moved to another neighborhood. We lost the house that Grandfather built in the mid 1930s and lived in five more houses in the remaining years in Holland. The first three were for three months apiece, as rental houses were sold from under us, and the next two we owned. In any event, the first of these was in "the country" on the edge of town and I felt neglected on Halloween, not having any friends about. Upon returning from some lonely trick-or-treating, I was surprised by a houseful of my buddies, and we had a fine time playing scary games among the haystacks and field mice under a bright moon. This was just one example of my parents' thoughtfulness.   ·

Travel

When I was five, Dad accepted the offer of a ride to Southern California to visit his parents and two youngest sisters in Glendale. He wrote an article on his travels for submission to the *Reader's Digest*, which, sadly, was not accepted. The highlight was a three-day return bus trip, which he survived though eating only the peach-jelly sandwiches that his sisters had prepared. At the conclusion of the ride, he was met by his brother Henry in Chicago and taken directly to a Cubs game ... that lasted seventeen innings.

Near another short-term house was Prospect Park, an unadorned meadow of about two city-blocks square. My dad would tell me that he would take me to the World's Fair when it came to Prospect Park. He did better, driving the family to the 1939 World's Fair in New York City. I enjoyed Billy Rose's Aquacade with swimmers Eleanor Holm and Johnny Weismueller and seeing the girl in the cake of ice (about thirty minutes?). We saw the Yankees play the Indians. My mother's two youngest sisters lived in New Jersey and it was a nice chance to see my four attractive cousins.

Our other major auto trip was to Chicago, where Dad's brother Henry was a high-school principal. Like my father, he had an M.A. degree in school administration from the University of Michigan. We saw the stockyards, the Museum of Science and Industry, Maxwell Street market, the Cubs, and Gary, Indiana.[8]

Sports

The town offered good sports facilities. One block away from our house were ten lighted tennis courts. Five of them were frozen over during the

---

8. Ten years later, the family took another drive to NYC. This time we walked down the middle of Broadway, with no moving vehicle in sight, to see the Rockettes, during NYC's all-time greatest snowstorm, of 1947.

long, cold winters for skating and hockey. A shanty with a potbelly stove was appreciated. In the summertime, several streets around town were closed for a block for roller-skating one night a week (when boys and girls hold hands), including the block directly in front of my house. The town supported summer-league softball at all ages. At age eleven, I was the town's boys' tennis champ; not many competed.

Bob Heyns told me he had read that the only position an average man could play in baseball's big leagues was "behind the plate." I responded that I was not average and would continue to try to follow in Lou Gehrig's steps, playing first base for the Yankees. The good omen was that we shared June 19 as our birthday. A drawback to overcome was that, although left-handed in finer things, I played baseball right-handed.

I reveled in the high school's winning the state Class C basketball championship both in 1934 and 1935. The finals for four classes were played on one day and we drove one hundred miles to sit through them all. Grand Rapids Christian won Class B in 1938 (coached by my Uncle Claus, husband of my dad's sister Harriet), so the regular New Year's Day contest between the two schools was a donnybrook. Games with nearby Zeeland were called off indefinitely because tensions were too high. In the final year, at Zeeland, my dad as timer shot a blank pistol to signal the end of the game when the concluding buzzer was not heard over the din. Unfortunately, he was sitting directly behind a shook-up police chief and spent a few hours in the Zeeland jail. One year I had the job of answering the phone at Kiefer's Restaurant, which was called by town-folks to learn the scores of away games.

A signal event took place when my class moved from grade school to seventh grade, housed in the high-school building. For the first time we had a gym and a coach. We had had the same playground basketball team for three years, as determined by "us five guys," who judged ourselves to be better players than the other ten or so boys in the class, with me as tacit captain. After watching us for five minutes, the coach benched me and made noises like I would stay there, commenting mostly that I wasn't aggressive enough. I was crushed; that action stunted my growth. What I figured out later was that I thought basketball was a half-court chesslike game, with set plays—true enough when there was a center jump after every basket made (or an outdoor half court in a driveway). But a year or so previously, the center jump was abolished and basketball converted to a full-court fast-break hurly-burly game, totally out of sync with my calm, deliberate style, mostly waiting for a teammate to feed me the ball. In candor, I suppose I didn't want to appear as if I were straining. The coach should have appreciated a "pure shooter." "Us five guys" minus me went to the state finals in their senior year—just imagine how much I would have liked to be with them. Dale Artz, Fred Brieve, Jerry Menken, and George Slikkers; I think Bobby Altena took my place.

Lasting Friends

My intention is to write about formative events, so I'll relate a lesson I learned in the second grade. When the class was to take a hike to visit Fred Brieve's dad's wholesale bakery, with boy-girl pairs holding hands, I approached the beautiful, serene Ruth De Graaf, confident that our understanding would cover this occasion. She informed me that she would be walking with Fred.

Later in the year, Fred and I were the student participants in a flash-card contest at a PTA meeting. I was a glutton for punishment and he beat me again. Actually, we were best friends and he was one of two classmates I managed to keep track of in adult years. At one point, he was appointed vice president of the Kettering Foundation (in Dayton, Ohio) at my recommendation; he had a Ph.D. in education and helped the foundation with a broad range of innovative programs.

I continue to be in touch with Rod Jellema who e-mailed me recently to say that he had run into a classmate who remembered a teacher saying that Rod and I were the only two junior-high students to read *TIME* magazine each week. Rod retired as professor of English Literature at the University of Maryland. I read his fine review of the tragi-comic novels of Peter De Vries, a Calvin graduate "whose works reflect his deep ambivalence toward the Christian faith." I see a dozen of De Vries's books on a nearby shelf. A large number of readers know that he is very funny, but they can't appreciate his best lines like we Dutch Calvinist boys do.[9] Rod remembers pretty little Tiny Ash. She once gave first aid to his wanderlust dog after the dog was hit by a car, and then wheeled him the six blocks to Rod's house in her doll buggy.

---

9. Another shelf reveals my not dissimilar John Updike collection.

Reunions

The Holland class I was in through junior high was the high-school graduating Class of 1946. It numbered approximately thirty students —about twenty-five of whom, I would guess, had been together since kindergarten. Come the fiftieth reunion, the organizers located me through a cousin and I was very happy to be invited and to attend, though I had moved away after the eighth grade and was living in Massachusetts. I took the opportunity to have dinner with Bob's wife Esther Heyns, then and now living in Holland. Marcia Van Tatenhove reminded me that she and I took our little red wagons to the renowned Baker furniture company to pick up scrap wood for use as kindling in our home furnaces—shades of the Depression.

The Tien reunion, held regularly during my youth at Tunnel Park on Lake Michigan, would draw about two hundred people. One attendee was (second) cousin Jim Wyngaarden, who became director of the National Institutes of Health (NIH). He and I would later review family history at annual meetings of the National Academy of Sciences. It was Jim who told me that we might have been wealthy had not our great grandfather lost a fortune on sugar-beet speculation.

The Swets clan would get together at the Lake Michigan cottage of the Cy Swets family. We were all familiar with a twenty-mile stretch of sand dunes running north from Holland. The large, public Ottawa Beach would often attract us shortly after dawn on the hottest days.

Prohibitions

There were two movie theaters in Holland, off-limits to me. I attended a show in one of them at age fourteen, after we had moved to Lansing and away from the glare of my dad's position in Holland, and when my parents were about ready to lift the ban. They were properly disappointed that I hadn't told them. "Devil cards" were prohibited in our circles, but not other card games (so "chance" wasn't the problem).

Tulips

I joined in Holland's annual Tulip Festival, now in its eightieth year. My first year I walked the mile-long parade route in wooden shoes; I vowed then to ride my (crepe-paper festooned) bike in future years. The town was especially beautiful the first week in May, with tulip lanes throughout and vast tulip farms on the edge of town. The town was festive, with bands and klompen dances and miniature Dutch villages and street scrubbing and concerts and trolley tours. Most of the citizens wore Dutch costumes through the week. I peddled Dutch babbelars (hard sugar candy) on the central corner of town and quit after one day with earnings of ten cents (net five cents after a soda).

Rod Jellema remembers that he and I were paid "big bucks" by Paramount News for modeling our Dutch costumes in Windmill Park. Years later he saw the film as a "short" at a naval base.

Adolescence

In closing this account of my early years, I confess my fascination in the seventh and eighth grades with Joyce. She was easily the best-looking girl I had ever seen, as blonde as befits a Dutch girl, aloof ("stuck up"), and a grade ahead of me. Painfully, my love went unrequited; I suppose it didn't help that I was tongue-tied in her vicinity. Some of my friends, unaccountably, were not that impressed; they would walk right up to her and say things like "Hi-Joyce-all-right-then." I see that my shyness turns out to provide bookends for this chapter; it must have been real. But stay tuned.

2 "P and that Stands for Pool"

"Trouble, oh we got trouble,
Right here in River City!
With a capital 'T'
That rhymes with 'P'
And that stands for pool."

– From the Broadway Production
The Music Man

If you stood on the front steps of the state capitol in Lansing, Michigan, and walked east down Michigan Avenue for two miles, you would come to the broad boulevard of Pennsylvania Avenue. Going left one block would bring you to Eastern High School. A bit farther and adjacent to the high school was Boys Vocational School (BVS), where twelve- to seventeen-year-old boys from across the state were committed for misdeeds. When Dad was appointed assistant superintendent of the BVS, after my eighth grade in Holland, I could look forward to living on the grounds of BVS and going to school at Eastern. Actually, I would be attending Pattengill Junior High the first year, for the ninth grade; it was nested into the L-shaped Eastern building. All were substantial institutions: I estimate 400 inmates and 600 and 1,200 students, respectively. The long corridor of Eastern seemed to require a bike, or at least a scooter; BVS grounds were a mile deep.

Of course, it's difficult for a youth to move to a new town. My parents made it easier for me by setting the first year as a trial and letting me drive back to Holland several times that year (I acquired a driver's license when we moved in June). Then I received a Valentine signed:

J.A.P.
(*guess who?*)

I was delighted to shift the focus of my Holland trips to Joyce. Also that spring, she and a mutual friend visited me for a weekend; a Lansing buddy of mine made it a foursome. All went smoothly for several months, but the ninety miles became an obstacle and we went our separate ways. The close of the trial year found me enjoying the new environment; the trial turned out, I suppose, the way my parents were pretty sure it would.

It was a pleasure beginning in the ninth grade to have a car at my disposal. Dad had a government-issue 1942 Chevrolet; Mom didn't drive, so I could have the family's 1939 Ford.

Boys Vocational School

Dad went to BVS with education and rehabilitation on his mind. The diverse population, however, didn't make it easy. It ranged from sophisticated seventeen-year olds from Detroit (or likely older, given that birth certificates were not always available to the court) to an eleven-year old from the Upper Peninsula caught stealing a chicken. The age issue came up when a winsome young lady appearing to be sixteen or so asked to be allowed to take her son Spaden Jones out for an afternoon furlough, the same Spaden we had thought of as about twenty.

My family lived on the BVS grounds for three years: one year in the assistant superintendent's residence and two in the superintendent's residence after Dad received a promotion. The second house was more commodious and enough closer to the high school that I could use the school's first bell as a wake-up call. I had the run of the place, including a key to the fieldhouse for some pick-up basketball games.

One day in the first house, I noticed about fifteen boys climbing the fence near our back yard, intent on escape. I called to Dad and we hopped in the car to intercept them at a point they would likely pass. As they reached us, Dad called out "FALL IN." They did! And he marched them in their familiar lockstep back to the school. There was not one thing he could have said or done differently and still achieved the desired effect. One misstep on his part and they would have been dis-

persed in the large woods just beyond us. He knew to depend on a stim-
ulus-response connection that the boys had made automatically several times a day.

Another event requiring decisive action centered on an inmate on
the recreation field who brandished a piece of pipe and a psychotic at-
titude to go with it; it was clear that anyone who ventured within his
reach was in mortal danger. After a standoff uncomfortably long, Dad
was located—without missing a step he walked up to the boy with his
hand outstretched. The young bucko handed him the pipe and they
walked off together.

Dad didn't always handle problems all alone; he had Charlie
Mirabeau. Charlie was an inmate who was handsome, gregarious, and
buffed. He could out-talk, out-run, out-smart, and out-anything anyone in the place. If he went to the starting line at a holiday track event,
no one else would contest. Charlie was unofficially "Trustee No. 1,"
but Dad would make use of his talents in selective ways. One qualifying situation arose when a low-wage employee was robbed of thirty
dollars in bills of various denominations. Dad knew the bills would
instantly be spread around to other inmates to make them difficult to
locate, and that only Charlie could retrieve them all in a matter of
minutes. He did, and nobody asked him from whom. So, the lore
about Charlie was reinforced without undermining his standing in
the inmate community.[1]

My Buddies

Starting in the ninth grade at Pattengill, I had many friends but five of us
developed a closer grouping. One day the phone rang in the gym office
and the instructor came out to the class and said "Denton [Don], go to
the principal's office." Then a second ring and "Nixon [Bob], go to the
principal's office." A slight pause and "Swets, you might as well go too."

As it happened, I wasn't involved in the shenanigans of the evening
before: a late party at the house of a girl whose parents weren't home.
And neither were Lou Hekhuis and Ron Runciman.

---

1. A friend of mine who read this chapter in draft mentioned that he thought the pris-
ons would be scarier places than I seemed to let on. They could be, but the inmates
knew when they had a friend in the front office. Sample: On his forty-seventh birthday,
the Ionia inmates had cake and gave Garrett Heyns a gold watch.

Bob Nixon passed away after a short practice of medicine and the four of us got together at our twenty-fifth class reunion; I came from Massachusetts, Don from North Carolina, Ron from California, and Lou from East Lansing. My son Steve, a student at Lawrence University in Wisconsin, took the opportunity to meet me half way. The guys thought it was great fun to regale Steve with tales of my wildest high-school high jinks—to his credit, he could not believe them. We had a golf tournament then and at the fiftieth reunion. I have a group picture taken at the fiftieth reminiscent of one in the high-school yearbook.

Sports

I had a good year in basketball in the ninth grade. In fact, many years later I received a certificate naming me as a member of Pattengill's Quarter-Century All-Star Team. I must mention that I was judged on a small sample of play: the war was on and constrained our schedule to two games. In one, I scored the first eight points in the first two minutes, and I'm hazy about the other, but it was good. My bench role established in the seventh grade took over again in high school. Friend-from-Holland-days Rod Jellema showed up behind the bench during an Eastern High game in Ann Arbor; his father was then in medical school there. I expected Rod to be in an A.A. uniform but he was in street clothes—'seems he was in arrears academically.

Our athletic conference was pretty good heartland: Ann Arbor, Battle Creek, Jackson, Kalamazoo, Lansing Eastern, and Lansing Sexton.

I outsmarted myself regarding baseball by thinking I could make the tennis team in my sophomore year but not be a regular on the baseball team. Jack Wickham offered to be my doubles partner and got me thinking about having three stripes on the sleeve of my senior letter sweater. Then another sophomore made the baseball team as a regular at first base—none other than my friend Lou—and I have thought ever since that I could have beaten him out for the position.[2]

On graduation day, Don introduced me to golf and I effectively turned in my tennis racket for a set of golf clubs that day. The pace of the game suited me better.

---

2. Lou sent me a note last month asking if I wanted him to say anything for me at the class's annual lunch meeting. I sent him a copy of this chapter and suggested he cull the paragraphs in which he is mentioned.

Elections

In the ninth grade, I was my homeroom's nominee for a citizenship award. I came in a close second and my homeroom teacher said if she had thought that could happen, she would have encouraged a unanimous vote for me from her room. In the tenth grade, several seniors urged me to run for student-council president. I lost to a senior, as I should have. In the eleventh grade, I was elected class president. In the twelfth grade, I lost the presidency to friend Lou, as I should have, not having distinguished myself in that role the year before. What's more, Lou has been student, professor, and dean of students at Michigan State University and hence available to handle our high-school class affairs since graduation from his home in East Lansing.

Academics

I found that I was quite good at geometry, and that when it came to algebra and trig, I just didn't have it. In geometry, the teacher would let me skip the five problems assigned (in the middle of the set) if I would do the last problem in the set. In algebra, it wasn't the ninth-grade teacher's fault, but the tenth-grade teacher didn't motivate me; so I couldn't handle calculus in college either. I learned in college that I was favoring "discrete" over "continuous" mathematics, and I got along fine then with such as set theory and probability theory—in general, the math of behavioral sciences rather than of engineering.

I was too lazy to take some courses that would broaden me, typing excepted. How I managed to win a scholarship to the University of Michigan plain escapes me. The scholarship waived tuition of $70 per term and led me to the university, despite the fact that my parents had moved into a house down the street from Calvin College.

Dramatics

In the ninth grade, the lure of greasepaint beckoned to Ron and me. We were recruited by the dramatics teacher to round out the cast of a forgettable "*WATCH OUT for SPOOKS!*" Ron was "Slats, a mischief maker," and I was "Randy, a friendly neighbor." Wild. Large auditorium. All in the way of personal development. I wish I could have relaxed. I still dream that I don't know my lines.

"T that Rhymes with P"

We boys played pool (pocket billiards), straight billiards, three-cushion billiards, and snooker pool, either at Pete's pool hall in downtown Lansing or at Steve's pool hall in East Lansing. At first we played outside of school hours. Then, when certain classes became too boring (one culprit was American History during the third hour just before lunch), our eyes would meet in passing in the hall and we would head for the door. We became better pool players (for money) than we were students, and naturally gravitated to our area of greatest accomplishment. I'm not proud of this, but one of us (not me) could imitate our homeroom teacher's signature on an excused-absence slip.

After two years of missing various classes, we came bounding out of Pete's one noon and bumped into our principal and assistant principal. They called us to the office after lunch and said that we had finally forced their hand and we were suspended from school. I went to my dad's office at the BVS to inform him and he said yes, he knew—the principals had given him the news over lunch at the Exchange Club. I can't remember but I imagine that the suspension was brief. Let's see, how does this play out: they won't let us go to school because we don't want to go to school?

However, I must implicate my dad in this lineage of disapproved, extra-curricular activities. Just today I came across (on the Internet) an issue of Spark, Calvin College's magazine, that featured a "flashback" to the Rivals, a student-run basketball team organized in 1920 that intended to represent the college before an official basketball program began. The group was frowned upon by college officials. When it consistently failed to submit the required copy of its constitution, the college suspended them. And so, back and forth, with various committee reviews and group non-compliances. On appeal, they were allowed to take exams, but not participate in Commencement. The article included a handsome group picture featuring Dad; I suspect he was one of the leaders.

To establish Dad's mischievous nature, I report that his deadpan visage appeared at both ends of the back row of his class yearbook picture. He had run end to end behind the group—faster than the panning camera.

Private Schools?

So, I was a public-school kid ... and happy in my innocence. I felt that my teachers and school administrators were intelligent, capable, and properly motivated, and possessing the resources they needed. It never came home to me that it was highly desirable, let alone crucially important, to attend the right prep school and then one of the top Ivy League colleges. I assumed that we lived in a meritocracy and good things would befall me as they were deserved.

It occurred to me later, however, that a culture of tutoring and individual development was lacking in my school, and I'll give one example. Friend Don performed exceptionally well in a standardized physics test and nothing was done about it. I could imagine his being approached by a physics teacher in a private school along these lines: "Don, let's find a time to meet weekly to discuss a physics book you will read. To get started: *Lives of Famous Physicists*. Next: *Advances in Physical Chemistry*. Then: *Physics Research at the Ford Motor Company*." Whatever.

Summers

Summers mixed jobs and sheer fun. I convinced a gas-station owner to hire me on my fourteenth birthday, the first day I could get a working permit, and lasted a day (forgetting to replace a gas cap). I spent the rest of that summer successfully filling orders in a paper-supply warehouse. At age sixteen, I spent a wonderful summer on Mackinac Island, the only greens keeper on the Grand Hotel's golf course. Several of my East Lansing friends were there, because the state parks commissioner lived in East Lansing, and we all bunked in the hotel's pool house. The governor's summer home was at the Fort and his daughter Joanne and I were an item—she invited me on a hayride—in a summer several items long.[3]

A memorable event at Mackinac Island was my taking out a horse to ride around the island, with insufficient previous experience. The horse learned soon that he was in control, and took me to the golf course to stomp around on the seventh green, doing a lot of damage. Did he know that I was going to have to repair it? When he was ready, he returned to the barn at high speed, sliding to a stop. The attendant said something like "Any fool knows not to bring in a horse like that." My excuse seemed clear: "*I* didn't bring in *the horse*."

---

3. I recently met Joanne's sister-in-law Jackie and mentioned that I had dated Joanne. Probably not a good word choice, because Jackie's e-mail to Joanne elicited the reply: "I don't know if I dated him or if he was just one of the boys I thought I might date."

The next summer I crated military chemical supplies, along with one student-athlete from each of the town's other three high schools, and was sent off the job the minute the news of VJ Day came through. That was okay because I had enough gas-rationing stamps to get to and from the Lake Michigan beach at Grand Haven, Mecca for people my age.

Senior Year

Dad and the commission that oversaw the BVS had some serious differences and came mutually to a parting of the ways at the end of my junior year. Uncle Garrett came over for dinner to discuss the situation and he and Dad asked me whether I thought Dad should write an editorial stating his views or go quietly. I said, "Rip 'em." Dad wrote a great piece for the *Lansing State Journal* (and saw his severance package reduced).

Dad and Mom settled in Grand Rapids and Dad went to work in real estate, quite successfully. I chose to finish high school in Lansing and stayed with the gracious Nixons. Uncle Garrett was working in Lansing, as the state's director of corrections, but he and Aunt Rosa had also settled in Grand Rapids; he and I drove back and forth together weekends.[4]

More Summer Jobs

Three more jobs, the summer after high school, each with a significant lesson. First, at Lansing's Fisher Body plant, I caught auto bodies coming off a line on wheeled platforms, one every thirty-five seconds, turned them around and pushed them onto another line running back—if I missed one, it ran into the paint shop and scared every one there. On day two, I was given a pail of rubber grommets and instructed to insert six on every body, to cushion the hood. On day three, I grew weary and pushed a red button to stop the line while I went to the men's room. The foreman came in and called "Swets, [expletive deleted], are you in here? I've got men sitting down for three miles. Here's your pink slip."

---

4. Now, during John McCain's "maverick" campaign for the presidency, I remember driving with Uncle Garrett to Southern Michigan Prison (in Jackson) where we toured the prison with Congressman Maury Maverick, Jr., grandson of the Texan who didn't brand his cattle.

In Grand Rapids then, I signed on at a construction site, where the first day I pushed wheelbarrows full of cement on 2 x 12 planks up and down to a bricklayer; the next day I couldn't get out of bed. The third day I swept cement dust off acres of new factory floor, most of it into my respiratory system. I made up my mind then and there to attend college. The next day, thanks to my dad's speaking to the foreman, I was given the plum job of driving a small truck around town doing pick-up and delivery. One day I cheated and stopped off at home for a bit, exactly when an emergency got my boss trying to track me down. I was fired and vowed never again to cheat on a (plum) job.

"With Your Hair a Raven Hue"[5]

I met Maxine ("Mickey") Crawford during our senior years at Eastern High; she had come from a different junior high than I had and it took awhile for those two student bodies to become acquainted. Then I never let her go. We're together now. We were married sixty years in 2009.

---

5. From the song "Mickey, Pretty Mickey"

3 "The Yellow and the Blue"

"Sing to the colors that float in the light,
hurrah for the yellow and the blue!
Yellow the stars as they ride through the night.
And reel in a rollicking crew.
Yellow the fields where ripens the grain,
and yellow the moon on the harvest wane.
Hail! Hail to the colors that float in the light —
hurrah for the yellow and the blue!"

– The University of Michigan song,
"The Yellow and the Blue"

I entered the University of Michigan in 1946 intending to study psychology. I arrived in Ann Arbor in the company of several friends from other Lansing schools and expected to be assigned with them to the freshman/sophomore West Quad (next to the Michigan Union which housed the pool tables). I found that the University staff handling orientation didn't have my name and the next morning I was assigned to the East Quad, populated by upper-class engineering majors. It was serendipitous, therefore, that one of them not only improved my bridge and table tennis games during my two years there, but also made a large contribution seven years later to my doctoral thesis. In all, I was at the University ten years: four as undergraduate, four as graduate student, and two as instructor and research associate.

Finding My Niche in Psychology

I intended to become a psychologist in order to help people and society. The major academic development in my first three years of college was finding that I did not know much about formal psychology and, specifically, totally coming to lose interest in two kinds of psychology I had earlier intended to pursue. My disillusionment came through participation as a subject in two experiments. First, I was disabused of the notion that I could learn to help individuals through 'clinical' psychology. Professor Jerry Blum's experiment presented pictures in a Rorschach-like, projective manner; his pictured character was a little dog named Blacky, and the experimental subjects had two minutes to write a short paragraph about each picture. The first picture surprised me, Blacky suckling his mother, and my story was almost nonexistent (I felt I had failed the test). I moved on to thinking I could help society with 'social' psychology. Professor Stan Schacter convinced me that I didn't care either for the social psychologist's bag of tricks; as a subject of his, I entered a structured discussion with a few other students who were later revealed to be hired stooges, manipulating me. The topic was the juvenile delinquent "Johnny Rocco" and I had been pleased to show my expertise.

In my senior year, Professor Don Lauer took me under his wing and hired me to assist in his 'physiological' experiment, which asked whether a dog could learn to make a conditioned response (leg lifting) even through a dose of curare prevented the response during training trials. Al Raphelson and I learned to implant a recording electrode on the leg's femoral nerve, to insert a catheter to deliver the curare in installments, and to artificially respire the dog.[1]

Then, in graduate school, I found 'sensory' psychology as the ultimately fastidious kind of psychology: in so-called threshold experiments, fully-informed human subjects press one or another button on each trial to indicate whether or not they had heard a weak tone, say, or had seen a weak spot of light. The resultant data are compared to various theories of sensory processes in 'mathematical' psychology. My version of a mathematical theory was also a 'cognitive,' as opposed to a 'behaviorist,' theory and remained at the center of my entire career. My interest was not in sensory systems for their own sake, but rather in using them as a pathway to studying the brain and mental phenomena.

---

1. I took "Christopher" home with me as a pet after the experiment—the first time I removed his leash, he wrapped himself around my ankle.

"Those Dear, Sincere Old College Days"

My years in Ann Arbor flew by. I loved the place. I was a member of the student council one year and chairman of its Political Action Committee, though not especially motivated along these lines at the university. I lived in a fraternity house (Sigma Alpha Epsilon) my junior year and enjoyed the easy sociability. We played a lot of paddleball; I think we enjoyed the bumping that four guys and four walls could do on a small indoor court. In my freshman year, I tried out for basketball and got a second look, but no more, from coach Ozzie Cowles. I was as avid a fan as any of Michigan football—and probably saw eighty games over ten years. I played basketball on the town-league team sponsored by the Washtenaw Dairy during my postgraduate years.

I admired my professors, especially John Shepard who taught the main, year-long psychology course. He set four essay tests during the year, each on a Saturday, that began at 8 am and lasted as long as anyone wanted to stay, usually not past 5 pm. Football players who missed the first exam, on a game day, could make it up on the Friday holiday after Thanksgiving Day. Students crammed day and night for three to four days before the tests, despite the course having taught them that *spaced* learning is far superior to *massed* learning. Lansing Sexton High friend Paul Gikas alerted me to this being the mother of all exams and became my fellow crammer. We memorized the 400-page textbook. After the test on sensory processes and perception, I proudly told anyone who would listen that I knew everything there was to know about the eye.

Bob Heyns was home from military service and on the faculty and I saw him and Esther occasionally. I asked him to suggest a topic for an English 1 theme and wrote on how science shouldn't be blamed for society's technological use of it. My professor liked my themes and told me that if I kept up the good work I could aspire to a grade of "B" in the course. That was a shock, but I supposed that the English department had to conserve its "A's" in case Arthur Miller should come along.

Mickey and I were married in the summer of 1949, at the Peoples' Church in East Lansing. Swets family members were pressed into service: Uncle Bill to officiate, Uncle Cy to sing, and cousin Jack as best man. Mickey and I took up residence in Ann Arbor. She took the position of secretary to the aeronautical engineering department and I spent the summer watering the university golf course, nights from 6 pm to 6 am. One morning walking home, I was picked up by the cops, who thought I had escaped from Ypsilanti's Hospital for the Criminally Insane. When the fall semester began, I took on a teaching assistantship in the undergraduate laboratory course.

The fire escape from our third-floor apartment was awkward and we were overjoyed when my parents helped us with a down payment on a house after a year. (It is gruesome to recall, but the apartment house burned down the next year, with a death in our apartment.) Our house was across town from the campus, and we got around in a twelve-year-old Pontiac. By this time, I had been accepted to the graduate psychology program at Michigan. A program, I might add, usually ranked in the top two or three in the country.

Graduate Study

I majored in the psychology of learning, which was the heart of theoretical and experimental psychology in those days. I pursued physiological psychology, with the highlights being the medical-school course in neuroanatomy taught by the eighty-year-old (at least) Elizabeth Crosby and a seminar on neural mechanisms led by psychology chair Don Marquis. I was interested in what could be learned about brain function from an analysis of language, stimulated by Karl Lashley. So I studied language in courses on phonetics and phonemics taught by Kenneth Pike and acoustic speech analysis as taught by Gordon Peterson. (I taught in the University's Summer Linguistic Institute headed by Pike. I had an offer of a professorship a decade later in Gordon's new communication sciences department, but elected to stay in Cambridge.) I took courses on sensory functions with Dick Blackwell, mathematical psychology with Clyde Coombs, and make-up mathematics with Bob Thrall of the mathematics department.

Friends

A group of we graduate students made life-long friendships. Included, with their professional destinations, are Robert Birney (Amherst, Hampshire, Williamsburg Colonial Foundation), William Dember (Cincinnati), Robert Earl (Claremont), Alfred Kristofferson (Cincinnati, McMaster), John Modrick (Honeywell Labs), and Alfred Raphelson (University of Michigan at Flint). In 1997, I gave a talk at a symposium honoring Bill Dember. A few years later, I had to miss a get-together of three of these friends in Ann Arbor. I've seen most of them singly right along.

This is the third group of close friends I've mentioned—one in each chapter. My magic number for the number of members in these groups seems to be six plus-or-minus one. There is the magical number seven in cognitive psychology—it's too bad I left social psychology before I found out if six is magic there.

Jobs

I generally held assistantships in the psychology department, but after the first year of graduate school, I took a summer job with the King-Seeley company, which had been making dashboards for Lincolns and Mercurys. At this time, it was making time fuses for bombs. The first day I stood over a vat of some horrible stuff (carbon tetrachoride?) cleaning metal parts. The next day I was shown a manual assembly line of some fifteen women, each with a machine to hone a little part to add to an intricate spring mechanism, and then passing it on. I was to keep each machine in tolerance to pass quality-control inspection. The assembly process was relatively new, so that piece rates had not been set. When the time-and-motion people came around, I managed to get favorable rates for the various tasks, so that the women could make good money. After a week, I was offered a job to watch over a half-dozen similar fifteen-person groups who were assembling other parts of the fuse. I resisted on two counts: I was still officially a "trucker" (my entry job category) earning the lowest wage and it was a night job, which I wasn't up for (our first child was just a few months old).

Fresh from a statistics course, I had been discussing sequential analysis with the quality-control representative to my assembly line and tried to get a transfer to that department. However, I ran into the policy that one could not transfer from production to quality control—one's sympathies would be suspect. I don't know how long the prohibition was supposed to last, or whether it would travel with me. The foreman said he would try to work something out if I would stay on, and not return to school in the fall.

In the fall, I took up an assistantship in the psychology department sponsored by the Ford Foundation. It fell under a project designed to bring together professors and students from several social sciences to attempt a multidisciplinary effort. The topic chosen was "conformity." The research was interesting and fun, but my interests lay elsewhere.

Once while working on conformity, I stopped by the physiological (surgery) lab to pick up a scalpel to trim a mat for a print I was framing at home. My buddies were there and as I was leaving, I heard a soft voice (I think it was Dember's but it might as well have been a chorus) say: "How the mighty have fallen!"

University Hospital

In ten years, Mickey and I used the University Hospital for three significant services, with interesting results. We would happily have missed the excess interest had we been able to use neighboring St. Joseph Hospital, equipped both for emergencies and routine services. First, as a college senior, I developed a case of acute appendicitis; the M.D. boyfriend of the nurse in the next apartment to ours rushed me to the hospital where I began to scream for a permission form to sign so that the cutting could proceed. The major hold-up was finding a physician at the University Hospital who could remember how to remove an appendix—this referral hospital did all of the fancy stuff, yes, but nothing mundane. No fooling, my operation was carried off by a physiology professor (with an M.D.); successfully, ... nice fellow.

In my tenth year in Ann Arbor, I reached to lift son Joe and tore a muscle in my lower back, left side. The right-side muscle missed its customary "reciprocal innervation" and clenched. A neighboring friend lugged me to the hospital—on New Year's Eve—where I was placed in traction. I found myself in a large ward with about fifteen young boys, sadly afflicted by chronic arthritis. As they wheeled themselves by my bed to check out the new (strange) guy, I realized that I had to sell them on the (strange) idea of tuning the one TV set in the room, the next afternoon, to the Rose Bowl channel, instead of their usual program. I tear up now, but they all agreed, having no idea what they were going to see, and resisting any sign of disappointment. We went on for ten days with me at the edge of their tight community; then, the mail boy delivered an envelope addressed to me as "Dr." —and the bloom was off the rose.

Our third hospital experience included two glorious events—the births of Steve and Joe. They were wonderful enough in themselves, but under the student medical plan, we got Steve for free and Joe for two bucks. True, the services offered were pretty sparse; we didn't know in advance, for example, who would deliver them.

Teaching and Sports

Two major teaching programs involved almost all of the graduate students as teaching fellows. The program for introductory psychology was directed for decades by Wilbert J. (Bill) McKeachie, internationally famous for that role. In my time, the program for the experimental psychology laboratory course was directed by Don Lauer. There were about fifteen and five teaching fellows, respectively, in the two courses. Don's fellows had less teaching responsibility per se and spent little time formally learning how to teach; I was one of them. It was great fun setting up an experiment each week, several of them classics in "brass instrument" psychology. Each week, the five of us assistants spent four hours putting together a ten-item multiple-choice test from the twenty-five or so items we had previously spent hours generating.

The two teaching programs had touch-football teams for the purpose of playing each other. Because Lauer's group could not field enough players, we recruited from elsewhere in the department. One year I recruited my pal Billy Raymond from outside of the department, from my fraternity in fact, who happened to be the University's all-sports champion (twenty-four out of twenty-five free throws, seventy for a round of golf, that sort of thing), not appreciating what a difference he could make as quarterback. Let's say I was chagrined by the lopsided score.

Bill McKeachie none-the-less continued to speak to me, possibly because I was his first baseman in the faculty's interdepartmental softball league. Bill's teams won the league title for years; he was a good enough pitcher to dominate the town league too. We typically beat Chemistry in the final game of the season, both teams unbeaten, by one run (or so it seemed). In our finest moment, we scored the winning run on a suicide-squeeze play, with me on third base and Spike Tanner batting. Spike and I had actually anticipated this play and I caught his signal. Another fond moment was Bill telling me after one season that I had finished with a higher batting average than he, the only person to do so in all his years.

Doctoral Thesis—Background

Wilson P. "Spike" Tanner, Jr., McKeachie's catcher, was a graduate student four or five years advanced beyond me. He and I discovered that we had common interests in a doctoral thesis topic. Spike took me to meet an engineer and a mathematician, both graduate students, who were working on a theory in electrical engineering that he and I thought might apply as well to human behavior. It was a theory of signal detection by mathematically ideal observers, for application in radar and sonar, but which gave promise of describing how humans detect weak stimuli, say, brief tones or spots of light, against a background of "noise" or random interference (or how, more generally, humans discriminate between two similar, confusable stimuli). The engineer was Wes Peterson, game-mentor friend from my freshman year at the East Quad; his colleague was Ted Birdsall.

They were part of the main laboratory in the electrical engineering department, called the Electronic Defense Group. This lab developed during the war with the support primarily of the U.S. Army Signal Corps.

As we began to examine the engineering theory, Spike and I decided to carry its terminology into psychology and we spoke of "signal detection theory," or "SDT," rather than, say, a new version of "psychophysical" theory. That was not an easy decision because, whatever argued for it, it helped to make us look to psychologists as coming out of left field. Psychologists were not accustomed to speaking of "signals" being detected against a background of "noise." Why call statistical variation "noise?"

The existing psychological (or psychophysical) theory for human sensory processes was accepted widely since Gustav Theodor Fechner proposed it in 1860, marking the origin of 'experimental' psychology. It incorporated a "sensory threshold," namely, a level of neural activity in the brain that had to be exceeded by the amount of neural activity arising from the stimulus in order for the stimulus to be sensed. This threshold was thus a physiological mechanism that operated in a fixed, predetermined manner to assign weak sensory inputs to one of two classes—sensed or not.

SDT conceived rather of a continuum of sensory inputs for a given stimulus, and a threshold that could be placed at any point along the continuum, of the observer's choice. This threshold would be considered a "response threshold," namely, a cutoff point determining the 'yes-no' response of the observer, rather than one dichotomizing the sensation level. (In SDT, the decision is "Yes, a signal is present," or "No, noise alone is present.")

The human observer would set a low threshold under some conditions or a high threshold under others, or one anywhere in between. A lower threshold (say "yes" more often) would be appropriate if the probability of the stimulus occurring were high, and conversely. In then-current psychological theory, the observer was to report whether he or she sensed the stimulus that was known to be present on every trial; in detection theory, the observer was to report whether a signal was present, knowing that it would be present only on some portion of the trials. The latter theory was appealingly more objective; the observer could be scored as correct or not.

In SDT, the choice of the threshold level would also depend on the benefits and costs of correct and incorrect decisions (true positive and true negative, false positive and false negative). For example, an observer would set a low threshold if the benefit of correctly reporting a signal as present (a true positive) were high while the cost of incorrectly reporting an absent signal as positive (a false positive) were low. The quantitative relationships between these variables were detailed in the electronic theory. They were originally specified in a statistical theory from which Peterson and Birdsall borrowed: the theory of statistical hypothesis testing, or statistical decision-making. The involvement of decision-making in the process made the theory one of the first 'cognitive' theories in psychology—that is, a type of theory setting aside the strictures of behaviorism in order to incorporate mental processes. This transition in psychology, after fifty years or so, is now pretty well complete.

The theory had attracted me immediately because I had been thinking about quantifying the instructions to the observer in order to fix the observer's mental set, principally the response threshold. In this line of thought, I had been examining the work of Clarence Graham at Columbia University, who had pointed up the need. SDT provided the way in one fell swoop: adjust the threshold by means of varying *probabilities* of signal occurrence or varying *benefits and costs* of the possible decision outcomes, or both. Those two variables mapped into the psychological variables of *expectancy* and *motivation* respectively. I began designing the experiments to validate the idea.

Spike and I were confident that the new theory could be experimentally established as valid for describing human processes, with significant consequences. We must have convinced Professors Bill Welch and Joe Boyd, who directed the engineering lab, for we were added to the payroll and moved into a hallway office in the East Engineering Building with Wes and Ted. We approached psychology professor Dick Blackwell to see if we could conduct experiments in his vision laboratory, it being the only facility on campus for sensory work, with him as thesis advisor and ultimately as chairman of our respective thesis committees. Dick and I agreed on some experiments; he and Spike did not at that time.

My experiments were strong tests comparing sensory-threshold and response-threshold theories and came out essentially the way Spike and I thought they would: the response theory was generously supported and the sensory theory was definitely rejected. Spike immediately wrote a short article he and I published in psychology's preeminent journal, the *Psychological Review* (in 1954).[2]

Thesis—Reaction from the Field

Fechner had claimed that his theoretical edifice would last forever because later investigators would not be able to agree on how to tear it down. It looked for awhile that Tanner and I would not be able to muster wide agreement on SDT, as many attempts were made to undermine it, but these attempts failed and adherents increased, and (as I write now), so far—so good.

Spike built an audition laboratory in the Electronic Defense Group, and our work there received careful scrutiny at meetings of the Acoustical Society of America. Our laboratory technical reports were disseminated selectively, which led to SDT being accepted in some quarters and resisted in others. It wasn't easy to overturn a one-hundred-year-old theory that many subscribed to and depended on in their own work. The different theories specified different experimental methods, again contributing to resistance to change. For example, resistance came from the Psycho-Acoustic Laboratory at Harvard University, led firmly by the venerable S. Smith Stevens. Acceptance came from two groups of psychologists that J. C. R. Licklider had recently assembled at MIT and MIT's Lincoln Laboratory. Spike's and my being affiliated with an engineering department didn't recommend us to classical psychologists, but was no drawback in the MIT complex. Elsewhere, mathematical psychologists Dick Atkinson and Duncan Luce thought it was important to consider theories alternative to SDT and proffered a few, but these theories were limited in fitting data.

---

2. The journal's editor was our friend Ted Newcomb; Ted's reviewer Harry Helson wrote "I don't know these guys, but they're on to something." Years later, I happily took part in a symposium honoring Helson.

A sidelight. Unsuspecting as I was, I submitted (in 1955) a manuscript based on my thesis to an associate editor of the *American Journal of Psychology* who happened to be a Harvard faculty member and associated with the Psycho-Acoustic Laboratory, Edwin B. Newman. He held on to it without an action decision for five years (read an exclamation point here). When I withdrew the manuscript, Dick Solomon, editor of the *Psychological Review*, offered to publish it, so it saw the light of day in 1961. I ran into "Eddie," as I had come to know him, about that time and he complimented me on the article and said he had assigned it to his class. That tickled me more, if that's the word, than the article's becoming a "Citation Classic."

Thesis—Reaction at Home

Dick Blackwell had an elaborate tome nearly completed on his version of a sensory threshold theory and wanted to make certain that it was not rendered passé by a new-comer theory (advanced by a couple of students). He refused to accept my first experiments as adequate for a doctoral thesis and required me to come back for another year to conduct additional experiments that he would design. I did that and drafted a dissertation in the spring, which he didn't get around to reading. When time was short, I submitted my dissertation to the graduate school without his approval. Dick reluctantly acceded to my having an oral exam after encouragement from department chair Don Marquis. He then dominated the exam, including answering questions from my committee that were addressed to me. Afterwards, the committee members apologized to me, individually, and Don instituted a new department rule stipulating that the thesis advisor could not also serve as chairman of the oral exam. My Ph.D. was awarded that June (1954).

Family

Son Stephen Arthur was born in 1951 and son Joel Brian, in 1954. In testament to my keeping studies in perspective, the first happy occasion coincided nearly with my master's comprehensive exam and the second with my doctoral orals. Maybe it was a matter of keeping up: although I had missed military service, many of my fellow graduate students were war veterans who arrived with families. Steve and Joe were fine boys. In college, they both majored in psychology before finding other fields.

As a matter of fact, I was not eligible for the draft because of the boys, and before that, because I was married. And before that, because I was enrolled in college. So, I kept one step ahead of the sergeant, as it were, unwittingly. Were I a month older, I would have gone to Detroit for an Army physical exam during my senior year in high school, facing a draft for WWII.

Final Two Years

In my final two, post-graduate, years at Michigan, I continued research in the electrical engineering department and teaching in psychology. Our group moved out of the hallway "office" into a new building on the North Campus, the Cooley Laboratories. My research replicated for audition the experiments done earlier in vision and added some that were better done in audition. I taught psychology of learning, language, and sensory functions. David Green, an undergraduate subject in one of my thesis experiments, entered graduate school, caught on fast, and joined Tanner and me in research.

The three of us began to write a broad technical report, entitled "*Some General Properties of the Hearing Mechanism*" (Technical Report 30 of the Electronic Defense Group). It should have been complete in six months, but took two years. We had grand arguments, which delayed matters. One time Dave read a draft in which Spike, in a mathematical development, had claimed that some theorem was "obvious." Dave came into our office stamping his feet and huffing and puffing ... and asking loudly "To whom the hell is this *obvious*?"

J. C. R. Licklider, psychology chair at MIT, came to visit our research lab in the summer of 1956 to see what these new people and their theory were all about. Actually, two investigators in his Lincoln Laboratory group had developed a similar theory. Shortly thereafter, he invited me to join the MIT faculty as assistant professor. I visited the MIT department while attending at MIT a one-week summer program on speech and language analysis (taught by luminaries Roman Jacobson, Noam Chomsky, Morris Halle, and Ken Stevens).

I also visited the psychology research group at Lincoln Lab and received an offer from Fred Frick to join it. I accepted the MIT faculty position. (Fred and I became good friends, and golfed together for decades.) Keith Smith, a classmate and friend at Michigan, had joined the Lincoln group two years earlier. When he was given the choice of moving to the faculty position or remaining at Lincoln, he chose the latter on the grounds that he preferred "two birds in the hand to one in the bush," his two birds being salary level and job security.

Mickey and I sold our house, packed the kids in a new station wagon, and headed east. We bought a new house in Lexington and she and the boys stayed with the Birneys in Amherst while it was being finished. Fortunately, Bob and Margaret had a college house large enough to handle the six kids. I stayed at the faculty club at MIT. (I spent one night under observation at the MIT Infirmary, to cope with a possible allergic reaction to penicillin taken for staph infection.)

The Green family also went to Cambridge that fall; Dave spent a year in the psychology department at MIT under a fellowship from the National Science Foundation.

Our house was delayed a bit and our family moved into the Licklider's house for a month, they being in California that summer. Our house was convenient to MIT by Rt. 2 and Memorial Drive, but I think the choice of Lexington was determined by a story that affected me when I was young, "The Little Minuteman." Here it is, abridged and lacking the original's suspense.

> A young Lexington boy was home alone one afternoon, awaiting his Minuteman father who would arrive at 5 o'clock, when he saw Redcoats approaching the house. He hid in the grandfather clock and listened while they searched the house, grumbling because they seem to have missed their man. They decided to wait until 5 o'clock for his possible return. It occurred to the boy that he might push the pendulum back and forth, gently to avoid detection, to make the clock strike five a little earlier. He did so for about an hour, painfully cramped, not making a sound, and the clock struck five at five minutes before five. As the Redcoats left, he heard his father come in the back door, safe and sound. He was "The Little Minuteman."

4   MIT and Psychology?

Birth of Cognitive Science

My move to MIT in September of 1956 was marked by a symposium at MIT that was said, first by Harvard psychologist George Miller and then by several historians, to contain most, if not all, of the core ideas of a new "cognitive science." This Second Symposium on Information Theory, sponsored by the Institute of Radio Engineers, included papers by Claude Shannon (information theory), Noam Chomsky (transformational grammars), Allan Newell and Herbert Simon (computers' discovering proofs of logic theorems), Ted Birdsall and me (a decision-making theory of human signal detection), and Miller himself (information capacity of human memory). Peterson and Birdsall, and Tanner and I, had given papers at the first such symposium, at MIT in 1954. Signal detection theory and information theory are closely related.

Tension

Peterson and Birdsall's 1954 paper was the first publication of their detection theory beyond a year-earlier technical report. To their surprise, a very similar paper was given at the same meeting by David Van Meter and David Middleton of MIT, who had received a copy of the technical report. Michigan professor Alan McNee rose to discuss the similarity, suggesting that the MIT paper copied the Michigan work, without attribution. MIT professors Jerry Wiesner and Walter Rosenblith strongly defended the integrity of the MIT authors. Middleton had been working on signal detection theory for several years, following in the path of the famous collection of scientists at the MIT Radiation Laboratory in the 1940s, especially A. J. F. Siegert, and Middleton's work was known and used by the Michigan authors.

When several of us convened at the Faculty Club that evening to sort out the matter, it developed that the MIT authors had taken some core ideas from the writings of the statistician Abraham Wald. Peterson and Birdsall had not read Wald and had developed those ideas on their own.[1]

Starting at MIT

J.C.R. Licklider wanted everyone to call him "Lick," and it was clear that for him "Joe" wouldn't do. When he and I met, he was moving from chair of the psychology section at MIT to a position with a research and consulting firm in Cambridge recently formed by three MIT professors, called "Bolt Beranek and Newman Inc." (BBN). He was leaving MIT because he felt that the administration was not following through with support for him to establish a graduate program in psychology.

BBN was founded as a partnership in 1948 to design the acoustics of the United Nations assembly hall. It was growing through consulting contracts in physical and architectural acoustics and in 1956 looked to Licklider to add psychological acoustics and work in "man-machine systems." Lick and Leo Beranek had been associated at Harvard and MIT.

During his transition, Lick hired Davis Howes and me into an otherwise depleted section. Davis, who had done his graduate study at Harvard, promptly did me two great favors. He pointed out that scientific papers could and should be written well and he suggested to his Harvard professor, editor Dick Solomon, that my thesis be published in the *Psychological Review*. His suggestion about writing, with a few examples where my paper could be improved, just flipped a switch in my head, and my writing immediately improved vastly. I rewrote the paper from

---

1. The fundamental ideas were the generality of the quantity "likelihood ratio," both as a measure of signal presence and a basis for describing all definitions of the optimal decision threshold.

scratch. It hadn't been that I couldn't write decently, but that I had accepted the notion that a concern for expression would tend to varnish and distort the scientific truth. Davis and I competed on the squash court and at the ping-pong table.

The psychology "section" at MIT was part of the "department" of economics and social sciences, so Davis and I reported to the department chair, an economist. He encouraged us to find a few more assistant professors to handle the teaching load in psychology, and we recruited Dave Green, my colleague at Michigan; Ron Melzack, a physiological psychologist from McGill; and Mike Wallach, a personality psychologist from Harvard. Meanwhile, another social sciences section appointed Roger Brown, a social/language psychologist from Michigan via Harvard. I had been a teaching assistant to Roger at Michigan and took over his psychology of language course when he left. The six of us lived in a figurative commune, with an economist watching over like a distant uncle.

There's a neat little story here. When I went, in September, to introduce myself to the economics department chair as his newest assistant professor, he didn't remember Lick's having told him anything about my appointment, or getting any approval for it. Lick was inclined, I found out, to gloss over administrative details and I had in writing only an ambiguous telegram from him. But the chairman said that any friend of Lick's was a friend of his, or words to that effect, and he would immediately make my appointment official. Moreover, because MIT was on a 1 July twelve-month basis for salaries, I could go to the bursar's office on the morrow and pick up my summer's pay.[2]

My acclimation was fairly easy, thanks to new friends. I took Bill McGill's position on the faculty and he left me his teaching notes for the introductory course, a course I had not taught. Thanks to Irv Pollack of the Air Force Cambridge Research Center, Bill also left behind his research contract, which Irv rewrote for my research, avoiding perhaps a year-long gap in research support. The administrators at the fabled Research Laboratory of Electronics (RLE) invited me to house my contract there and let them manage its contractual and financial affairs.

---

2. A far cry from the way position openings are advertised, and applicants vetted, nowadays.

I moved into a paneled office in the Sloan Building, formerly the head-quarters of Lever Brothers, with a view of the Charles River and the Boston skyline. My lab was on a well-furbished lower level. The Institute's faculty club was on the sixth floor. Lick left a ping-pong table in his lab.[3]

Teaching at MIT

MIT was an academic's dream. A professor was permitted to "buy back" up to half of his or her time, by paying salary from a research contract. The Institute required teaching one three-hour course for its contribution of half-time salary. I taught introductory psychology a few times and the courses I had developed at Michigan. The "intro" course was purely lectures to about 150 students—with no graduate assistants to conduct discussion sessions. I set a practice of lecturing without notes, which I felt improved the presentation noticeably.

Students

About a dozen students comprised my freshman advisees group each year. They would come out to our Lexington home for a casual gathering during orientation week. One year I noted the contrast between a prototypical MIT student who had prepared at the Bronx High School of Science and a student from upper Maine who had apparently gotten to the wrong institution. The Bronx grad talked to me about his advanced courses, while the Maine boy spoke about his late evenings of poker. To my great surprise, the first didn't survive the first semester and the second finished the first year with passing grades.

Uncle Garrett called me to ask if I would explore the admission by MIT of one of his Michigan-reformatory inmates. I pompously suggested considering a school like Purdue, which emphasized practical engineering over abstract science. I learned later that this inmate received an advanced degree in pure mathematics. Just an example of the stupidities I mostly suppress in thinking back.

---

3. Thinking of that building brings to mind a talk given there by Jimmy Hoffa to twenty or so invited faculty. The industrial relations section was his host; I can't recall why I was invited. What was memorable was Hoffa jumping up on a large conference table and vigorously addressing his ringed audience for an hour while in constant motion.

The Netherlands

I was invited to spend the summer of 1958 at the Institute for Perception Research, sponsored by the Philips company, and directed by Jan Schouten in Eindhoven, The Netherlands. Ken Stevens from MIT had spent the previous summer there and gave a good recommendation to Mrs. Veldhorst's room and board. The Swets family, with boys aged seven and four, had a grand time, with the boys handling the new language better than their parents. Side trips were made most weekends, in the Netherlands to tulip and cheese centers and to the frozen-in-time villages of Spakenburg and Bunschoten; and also to Brussels (the Expo) and down the Rhine to Cologne. We visited denBosch, where my Grandfather Heyns had spent his army time. The ocean voyages were wild: the outgoing trip in a cabin across from the cocktail lounge, so we heard lusty choruses of "Ein, Zwei, Zufall" and "Mack the Knife" almost all night; and the return trip in a shallow-bottomed boat with no cargo on its first trip outside of the Indies, so the side-to-side swing had about a five-minute cycle.

We picked up the return ship in Le Havre, permitting a couple days in Paris; no other city in my travels has thrilled me half as much. The value of having friends at RLE was demonstrated: earlier I sent the financial officer a cable requesting $80 to travel to Donald Broadbent's lab in Cambridge, England; the dollar figure was garbled in the transmission so he sent me $500. As it turned out, I needed every penny of that to get the family back to the States. My summer's research results turned out not to justify independent publication, but were included in a later survey article.

BBN Inc.

MIT permitted a day-per-week of outside work ("consulting"). I spent my time during the first two years at Melpar Corporation, with the MIT detection theorist Dave Van Meter. I signed up with Lick at BBN in fall 1958. Dave Green was there in his first faculty year at MIT. We contributed to on-going projects and I wrote a proposal for my own research.

My proposal was to develop a computer-based laboratory for research on perception and learning. The computer would generate auditory stimuli, control the trials, accept responses from human subjects, interact differently with different subjects depending on responses, and analyze data—everything but write the report. In one mode, the computer would act as a "teaching machine." BBN had the only computer available at the time capable of such functions—the prototype version and then the first production model of the PDP-1 from the Digital Equipment Corporation. ("PDP" stood for Programmed Data Processor at a time when the government issued a moratorium on buying "computers.")

Societies

Tanner, Green, and I linked up with the Acoustical Society of America (ASA), through Lick's auspices. (His daughter Linda thought there was a single person named "Tannerswets'n'green.") We went to two four-day meetings a year, published in the journal *JASA*, and stayed up half the night at meetings to argue technical issues. I assumed that it was Lick's doing when I was elected a Fellow in 1959. At age thirty-one, I was the youngest ASA fellow by several years; the elevation was no doubt premature, but Lick was not much for custom. Also, he had a generous view of the people he knew—maybe because, as Bill McGill said, talking with Lick raised one's own IQ by thirty points.

I followed Lick as chair of the Society's Technical Committee on Psychological and Physiological Acoustics, each of us for three-year terms. At each meeting of the society, on one evening an open meeting of members in that technical specialty was followed, ostensibly, by a closed meeting of the committee in the chair's suite. However, the chair would deem the open meeting to have handled all the business, so the committee members and others of like mind were free to socialize during the "closed" meeting (with beverages charged to BBN). And socialize they did, unforgettably, 'til the wee hours.

A second society, called PRT for "Psychological Round Table," consisted of east-coast psychologists who joined by invitation. They were "superannuated" at age forty, the approximate age at which they might be invited to join the Society of Experimental Psychologists (SEP), our profession's leading honorary group. For a bit, PRT considered mocking SEP by calling itself the Society of Experiment*ing* Psychologists. I joined PRT in my first year at MIT and Dave Green joined a couple of years later. A distinctive feature of this organization was that the chair called on speakers in any order, with no warning. Speakers had trouble finishing amid the humorous jibes. The banquet talk was always pretty wild. The group was run autocratically by a committee of six rotating members. I took a turn. The group would meet on a weekend, taking over a country inn. It was understood that members would not list the PRT on their curriculum vita. The society began admitting women in the 1960s.

"Society" is too formal for the third group of interest, consisting of about twenty Cambridge area psychologists (mainly from MIT, Lincoln Lab, Harvard) who met monthly in season for dinner at the MIT faculty club and a talk by one of the group on work in progress. It was called "The Pretzel Twist."

Symposia and Publications

In 1960, I spoke at the Fechner Centennial Symposium in Chicago and at the Fourth London Symposium on Information Theory. Both talks were published in 1961. Also in 1961, I published my thesis with Tanner and Birdsall in the *Psychological Review,* as mentioned earlier, and another major article in *Science* magazine. The latter article was partly in response to a *Science* article in 1960 by S. S. "Smitty" Stevens, founder and head of Harvard's Psycho-Acoustic Laboratory, entitled "Is There a Quantal Threshold?" the "quantal" threshold being his version of a sensory threshold. He wrote his article in reaction to a Cambridge meeting in which SDT was viewed approvingly by several attendees. I was a little cute, calling my article "Is There a Sensory Threshold?"—the implication being, let alone a quantal sensory threshold. Meanwhile, I published four articles in *JASA.*

Dave Green and I presented a paper jointly at the London conference. He used support from the National Science Foundation to get a commercial airline ticket that gave him a six- or seven-hour jet flight. With my support from the Air Force, I was at the mercy of the Military Air Transport Service. I flew from Boston to Philadelphia, took some land conveyance to McGuire Air Force Base in New Jersey, took a propeller plane that flew over Boston ten hours after I left it, refueled in Iceland and Prestwick, flew to Mildenhall for a two-hour bus ride to London—elapsed time of thirty-nine hours.

Summer Program

I arranged a one-week summer program at MIT in 1962 to present a survey of signal detection theory in psychology. A dozen or so people gave talks to forty to fifty attendees and Lick spoke at the banquet. Ar-

ticles collected as class notes for the course and a few others were assembled in a book I edited in 1964, called "Signal Detection and Recognition by Human Observers." The book became a "Citation Classic."

MIT Does Its Thing

We left MIT's psychology program at the outset of this chapter with five
assistant professors and one full professor (Roger Brown), no chairman,
and no graduate program. Davis Howes and I were named associate professors in 1960, albeit without tenure, which at MIT was considered only for individuals who had reached thirty-five years of age. We all felt we
needed some structural enhancements of psychology at MIT in order to
have an identity and some stability at a primarily technical school.

There had been several attempts over twenty years to establish a psychology graduate program at MIT, beginning with a group of Gestalt
psychologists assembled by the highly regarded Kurt Lewin. Sometimes, the thrust came out of the School of Industrial Management,
sometimes the School of Humanities, sometimes the Department of
Economics and Social Sciences, all watched warily by the School of Engineering. In later years, the psychology research group at MIT's Lincoln Lab was a potential asset, as were linguists and physiologists in the
Research Laboratory of Electronics. However, the MIT administration
was never encouraged enough to take on the financial responsibility.
Incidentally, Don Marquis, chair at Michigan, was the outside advisor
most sought in these deliberations; at this point, in the late 1950s, he
was a professor in MIT's School of Industrial Management.

In my fourth year at MIT, a new chair of the economics department,
Bob Bishop (a golfing pal), was willing to hire a senior professor of psychology who ultimately, if circumstances permitted, would head a new
psychology department including a graduate program. We six staff
made a list of candidates and presented it to our economics chair, who
discussed it with other interested parties at MIT. In the end, we all settled on someone hardly known at MIT, Hans-Lukas Teuber from New
York University, and primarily its affiliated medical school.

Surprisingly to us, Teuber turned out to be interested exclusively in
faculty who worked in his specialty—the relationship of brain and behavior. He himself studied brain damage and loss of function. Even
more stunning, he stood off all of the interested parties on campus until they gave up on the idea of participating in the new department. The

six of us in the core group he inherited left MIT within a year or two. Spread to the winds: Harvard, McGill, Pennsylvania, Duke, Boston University Medical School, and BBN. It was sad: MIT could have collected twenty or so of its staff to be one of the top psychology departments in the country overnight. (And I'm not the least bit worried about exaggerating here.)

My Move

I went to BBN full time in 1962, on a leave of absence to fill in for Lick who was going on leave to the Advanced Research Projects Agency of the Department of Defense. Lick did not return to BBN and I did not return to MIT. He saw an opportunity, on a national scale, to develop computers and computer networks capable of "symbiotic" relations with humans. Less grandly, I saw a chance to do research full time, applied as well as basic research, in a congenial environment (no committees, no arguments about lab space, no faculty politics). Also, the applied research added something more humanitarian to psychophysics.

I inherited a project on "Libraries of the Future" and another on a computer-based teaching machine for rote learning (for example, foreign-language vocabulary). Under the latter project, I took advantage of the new PDP-1 computer to develop a computer system for learning under an interactive, conversational (Socratic) method, applied primarily to medical diagnosis.

Whither My Fan Club?

BBN and the psychology profession were congenial to me for the remainder of my career, as illustrated in following chapters. So I can sum up the conclusion of the various adversarial positions taken by various senior people at the outset of my career. Thesis advisor Dick Blackwell and I met at a professional session in Cambridge; he told me of an article he was writing to compare his theory to mine and I let bygones be bygones, given that the relative status of those theories had by then been pretty well settled. A few years later, Dick moved to Ohio State University and at about the same time Ohio State University's Professor Paul Fitts moved to the University of Michigan. I complimented Michigan's vice president Bob Heyns on the trade and he replied: "We threw in the stadium."

Editor Edwin Newman, as I mentioned, seemed to forget his delay in considering my thesis as submitted to his journal, and I let it ride. Smitty Stevens and I became friendly when I spent several evenings in his home working with his wife, Geraldine known as "Didi," proof-reading my first book. He gave me a copy of his "Notes for a Life Story" with the inscription "Warm greetings!" I think I made the overture to Smitty by telling mutual friend Leo Beranek that we detection theorists argued so vigorously with him that he probably didn't realize how much we respected him. He served on a committee I chaired for the Federal Aviation Administration on "Human Response to Sonic Booms."

H.-L. Teuber and I met again but once, when I gave a colloquium at his department (I think some of his new staff were curious about their predecessors). He displayed his disinterest in my work by writing in his first annual report that I had published an article entitled "Is There an Information Theory?" (his version of my article "Is There a Sensory Threshold?").

The last antagonist to mention was Walter Rosenblith, who was on the MIT electrical-engineering staff after moving from Harvard's Psycho-Acoustic Lab. He came in late to a talk I was giving at MIT's Research Laboratory of Electronics, interrupted to harangue my work for several minutes, and then said he had to leave for an appointment with a student. Walter later subsided and was the first to write me a congratulatory note when I was elected to a national academy. Walter even took Spike Tanner's and my side in a technical debate with his colleague Smitty. When Teuber's report came out, I consoled Walter by writing him: "Yes, Virginia, There is an Information Theory." Judi Rosenblith sent me a copy of the program from the MIT memorial for Walter with a warm note.

All in all, the foregoing is an amazing tale of hostility to befall a quiet, unassuming fellow and I'm sure none of it was personal. If I didn't realize at first that Spike and I were on to something with our research, the intensity of these reactions made it clear. It no doubt hurt plenty to be upstaged by a couple of guys out of nowhere. Besides that, MIT was the home of detection research before Peterson and Birdsall entered the field, and the Harvard folks didn't pick up on its relevance. Fortunately, fences were mended. I do wonder though what it might have been like to move to Cambridge without having to fight its mandarins. As the reader will have inferred, my parents reared me to move "toward" or "with" people (as characterized by the psychoanalyst Karen Horney)—not "against" people—and they didn't try to give me any fighting skills.

The Arie and Kate Swets Family. Dad (John) is in the middle.

The William and Hendrika Heyns family. Mom (Sara) is at left.

Mom and Dad Swets.

Aunt Rosa and Uncle Garrett Heyns.

Uncle Seymour and Aunt Wilma Swets and Family.

Left: With great friend Mina "Tiny" Ash.
Right: With sister Mary Lou, lacking wooden shoes.

My family at the warden's residence at Michigan Reformatory.

*High school buddies. Back row: Lou Hekhuis, William Sage (a teacher),
Don Denton. Front row: Ron Runciman, John Swets, Bob Nixon.*

Greenskeeper, Grand Hotel golf course, on Mackinac Island.

Number 3, with high school team.

Boys Vocational School.
The public schools are in the lower right corner.

Psychology graduate students at the University of Michigan (Bob Earl, Al Raphelson, Andy Karoly, and John Swets) with three-dimensional rat maze.

Committee on Techniques for the Enhancement of Human Performance, of the National Research Council, at a meeting in San Diego. From left: Gerald Davison, Robert Bjork, Michael Posner, Ray Hyman, Walter Schneider, John Swets, Daniel Landers, Sandra Mobley, Lyman Porter, Daniel Druckman, Lloyd Humphreys, Richard Thompson, Sally Springer, Jerome Singer.

With an advanced input–output computer system at BBN in 1963.

With David Green in BBN's PDP-8 computer-based laboratory
for the study of signal detection.

With "The BBN Authors' Shelf."

"The Boys" posing at Notre Dame.

John lays a rock ... Mickey sweeps a rock.

With son Joe at Royal Troon Golf Club, Prestwick, Scotland.

Steve, Michael, Diana, and Caroline Swets,
at the 2009 Boston College Commencement.

Mickey and John on Nantucket Island.

5 BBN: "We'll Solve *Our* Problems"

Probably the oldest and best-known technical consulting and research company in the U.S. is the Cambridge firm Arthur D. Little, Inc. Their motto has been:

Send us your problems and we'll solve them.

Upstart Bolt Beranek and Newman Inc. (BBN) came along about six decades later and was said to have a contrasting motto:

Send us your money and we'll solve *our* problems.

The statement attributed to BBN captures nicely its cockiness, and is supported by its performance. When I was at BBN, the company had roughly 200 to 400 research contracts at any one time and I estimate that half of them were based on unsolicited ideas of BBN scientists and engineers.

Indeed, scientists often came to work at BBN as entrepreneurs. They brought their ideas and the company supplied other essentials, for example, contracts and financial expertise, space, equipment, and assistants—not unlike professors.

BBN's research contracts (and some grants) were supported largely by government agencies, for example, research offices of the Department of Defense, institutes of the National Institutes of Health, and divisions of the National Science Foundation. For these funds especially, BBN competed with universities and other nonprofit organizations, and fared well in the competition despite higher costs. The various types of organizations were similar enough in their academic outlook that BBN was sometimes called "Cambridge's third university." A large proportion of BBNers held advanced degrees and some doctoral theses submitted to local universities were carried out at BBN. In addition to *research*, about one-tenth of BBN's business was *consulting* and another tenth, *development*, which led to products and services. The major fields were acoustics, psychology, and computers—independently and in interaction. I'll point out later how these three fields came to be at BBN.

I joined BBN part-time in 1958 and full-time in 1962, and remained there until 1998, when I went on *emeritus* status (retired with privileges) at age seventy. (I was Employee No. 158; there were only two or three employees left with a lower number when I retired.) My time at BBN divided into three phases: (1) for about twelve years I conducted research; (2) then for five years I managed the consulting, research, and development (CRD) activities; and (3) in the final twenty-plus years I did research and at times led a staff-development program. This chapter tells something of those forty years, except for my primary research in the third phase—on medical imaging—which is the subject of the next chapter.

Job Titles

Although I called my first BBN phase "research," accurately enough, for most of that time I was vice president of BBN and codirector of the Information Science and Technology Division, which included psychology and computers. The reason for this anomaly was that President Leo Beranek thought the other "co," Jerry Elkind, and I had identified each other as rivals, and that it was important to treat us alike. Hence, when Jerry, who wanted to be a manager, received a promotion, I, who did not want to be a manager, received the same. Jerry and I worked things out amicably: he did all the management. (I don't mean to disparage management; I just thought of myself as a professor.)

I did help Jerry occasionally, for example, with annual reviews of staff. Bob Kahn, who gets "co" credit with Vin Cerf for spawning the Internet, reminded me a few years ago that I gave him his first review at BBN. He remembered that when I asked him what he had accomplished, and he said, "Well, with mathematics, it's sometimes hard to know," I replied that if he didn't know then I surely didn't, and he would not get a pay raise. I don't recall if we left it at that.

Later, I was persuaded to become a real manager, to be called general manager of BBN and senior vice president, and to oversee the technical side of the company. (The financial side, including contracts and investments, was in the hands of another senior vice president.) The persuasion took place at a gathering of the Board of Directors at Dick Bolt's house and I was invited to join the board. The company had just been through an aborted merger, leaving the troops unhappy, and I think I was seen as a healer. Jerry had left the company in the throes of the merger to manage the computer activities of Xerox PARC (Palo Alto Research Center). In hindsight, whether I became a "real" manager at that time might be debated: I continued with many technical activities during those years, including writing an article for *Science* on the current state of detection theory and its growing number of applications. In any case, the five division directors reported to me—contentedly, as far as I could tell.

Not that these were placid times. For example, BBN had an active chapter of *Science for the People*, which enjoyed protesting and disrupting a symposium of a Boston meeting of the American Association for the Advancement of Science, being chaired by BBN chairman Dick Bolt.

My last title was chief scientist for the information sciences. At the same time, Jim Barger, then a division director, was appointed chief scientist for the physical sciences. We oversaw the promotions of staff along a newly defined technical career path and chaired the group of about a dozen "principal scientists" at the path's top level (in a job category with the perquisite of a five-month sabbatical leave every five years). We also directed a staff-enhancement activity called the "Science Development Program." In a turnabout from my arrangement with Elkind, this time Jim had better things to do and I took on the greater share of our administrative responsibilities.[1]

Information Retrieval

When Lick left me a project on "Libraries of the Future," I took the opportunity to carry out research on the application of signal detection theory (SDT) to measuring the effectiveness, or accuracy, of informa-

---

1. To exemplify the point that Jim could justifiably focus on technical activities, many years later a project he inspired to develop an antisniper device to pinpoint a sniper's location from a moving vehicle led in 2008 to a seventy-four million-dollar order from the Army for some 8,000 of the devices—BBN's largest contract to date.)

tion-retrieval systems. (In general, an "IR" system retrieves desired "items"—the items could be documents, abstracts, answers to questions, and so on.) I was able to show in a *Science* article that the ten accuracy measures then used in the field confounded the accuracy of retrieval with the willingness of a system to yield items—a problem SDT alone solves.

In a review of three large retrieval studies conducted at three different institutions (they kindly lent me their data), I highlighted the inherent difficulty of the retrieval problem in an article in *American Documentation*. Assume a collection of three thousand items of which ten are relevant to the query at hand. For the most accurate systems available, retrieving on average nine of the ten relevant items would bring on average three hundred irrelevant items mixed with them. To reduce the number of such "false drops" to, say, thirty, by means of a strict threshold for retrieval, one would receive only four of the ten relevant items.

(Lick, you may imagine, disappointed the Ford Foundation's Council on Library Resources when he left the project. The Council had convened a blue-ribbon panel to identify the person best qualified to head the project, which settled unanimously on him. He recovered to a large extent by writing a final report that became the book *Libraries of the Future*, which is seen as shaping many of the central concepts of the online information commons of today.)

Bulletin! The Receiver Operating Characteristic, or "ROC"

I say "Bulletin!" because I need my dear readers' attention here to something slightly technical and quantitative—an analytical technique of SDT that is central to most of the research applying the theory and its methods.

This analytical technique is a graph showing how the proportions (or probabilities) of "true positives" and "false positives" vary together—for a detection or diagnostic device of any given accuracy—as the decision threshold is varied. Figure 1 shows true positives on the Y-axis and false positives on the X-axis—with both proportions ranging from 0 to 1—and a single illustrative curve. As hinted by my remarks about information retrieval, when true positives increase, so do false positives, and the other way around. A lenient threshold for a positive decision leads to high proportions of both true and false positives (near the upper right corner) and a strict threshold leads to low values of both (near the lower

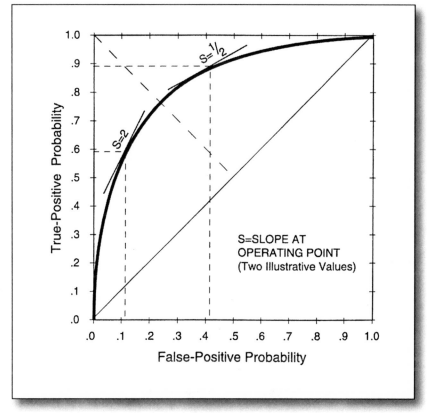

Figure 1.

left corner). The graph is a concave arc from lower left to upper right.

The graph is called the "receiver operating characteristic," or "ROC" (pronounced as spelled: "are-oh-see"). The graph gives a measure of detection *accuracy* (or diagnostic accuracy) and a separate measure of the decision *threshold*. (The "decision threshold" was termed a "response threshold" when I discussed human performance earlier, but "decision" is the more general term.) Accuracy is reflected in the height of the ROC curve: a higher curve will have a higher proportion of true positives for any given proportion of false positives. Figure 2 shows four curves, illustrative of different accuracies. The threshold is reflected in the location of its point along a curve; a point near the lower left represents a stricter threshold than one to its right. Figure 1 shows two illustrative threshold points.

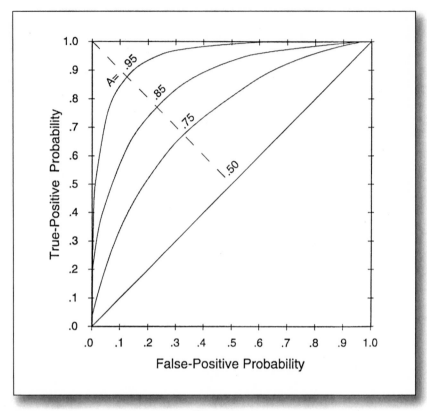

Figure 2.

A convenient measure of *accuracy* is the proportion of area of the ROC square that lies beneath the curve—designated "A" in figure 2. This value ranges from 0.50 (for a curve along the diagonal, giving zero or chance accuracy) to 1.00 (for a curve running along the left and top axes.) A common measure of the *threshold* is the slope of the ROC curve at the point the threshold produces (decreasing as the curve extends from left to right). Figure 1 shows two values of the slope "*S*." The *optimal* value of *S* for the situation at hand can be calculated from the

---

2. I once tried to change the name of the ROC to "*relative* operating characteristic" when it started to become clear how far from receivers it would take us, but the new terminology didn't catch on. I even used "relative" in the title of a *Science* article. It was a term that Ted Birdsall suggested for technical reasons I won't go into.

benefits of the correct decisions and the costs of the incorrect decisions and the probabilities of the two possible events.[2]

The ROC has been widely applied in psychology, for example, to recognition memory and other cognitive abilities—any time fine discriminations are required. Jim Egan first applied the ROC in psychology to problems other than sensory processes, namely, to vigilance and to recognition memory. Jim was a professor at Indiana University and a friend of the Michigan contingent through meetings of the Acoustical Society.

The ROC has been widely applied in other scientific fields to measure detection or discrimination, and also in several applied fields to evaluate diagnostic devices—that is, common, practical devices that attempt to distinguish positive items or conditions from negative ones, such as x-rays and models for weather prediction. The application to information retrieval just described was the first application to a diagnostic device and paved the way for the more general usage in diagnosis.

Having introduced the ROC, let's return for a moment to my substantive point in the *American Documentation* article, namely, that information retrieval is inherently a very difficult problem. In reprinting the article in *Key Papers in Information Science,* Belver Griffith emphasized the point:

> [Information retrieval] is, of course, a perennial topic within information science, and some would say it is the core of the discipline. The past few years, beginning with Swets' article, show this to be an area of increasing empirical difficulties. This critically important article is not included as an endorsement of his theoretical model, but rather as an indication of the difficulties in doing this research. In particular, one should note Swets' argument in identifying the best operating characteristic curve for information retrieval systems. Considering that argument, is there an absolute and quite low threshold [ceiling] for the effectiveness of these systems?

The ROC is now ubiquitous, especially in medicine. Yahoo shows about six million results. More on this topic as we go along, as I describe how my doctoral-thesis ideas continued to command my attention, but first a few other happenings during my early BBN years.

Computer-Assisted Instruction

In the late 1950s, B. F. Skinner popularized the "teaching machine," which implemented the principles of "programmed instruction"—such as continual interrogation and overt response, immediate knowledge of results, learner-controlled pacing of the lesson, and presentation of successive items conditional upon previous performance. Others appreciated that a computer would provide an effective way of employing those principles, but the other computers available were no match for the PDP-1 then at BBN. In a task requiring a learner to associate arbitrary names with nonverbal sounds, I compared the Skinner method to a simple pairing of the sound and its name, without overt response—and found the simpler method to yield faster learning. The experiment and results were published in the *Journal of the Acoustical Society of America*; a journal in applied psychology would have been a better choice.

The PDP-1 was versatile enough to suggest an "intelligent tutor." And I managed to redirect another project that Lick left me to this topic. I arranged with BBN department manager Tom Marill to hire computer-scientist Wallace Feurzeig to help me develop a "Socratic System" for teaching diagnostic skills, say, in medicine. The student was given a small vocabulary of questions and declarative statements (about thirty-five each). The computer would respond to any of them with an answer, a comment, or a question. Either computer or student could take the initiative. The computer's contributions depended on the student's actions up to that point, and on their order. The patient's condition and the computer's responses to a given question could vary over time. The computer could answer good questions, reprove hasty conclusions, question the grounds of inference, and suggest new approaches. Wally and I published an article in *Science* in 1965 describing what some termed the "grandfather of intelligent tutors." Other articles appeared in the *Journal of Medical Education* and *Datamation*.

Wally went on to an illustrious career at BBN as an international leader in computer-assisted learning, and is active in that role as I write this.

Lick would not give any contracts to BBN from his post at the Advanced Research Projects Agency, cutting off BBN from the major source of support for the kind of computer research it was doing. After Lick's term there concluded, ARPA invited me to submit a proposal and accepted my proposal to develop computer techniques for teaching a second language, including its pronunciation as well as its syntax and semantics. The machine made an acoustic analysis of a student's utterance in real time and displayed visually any serious discrepancy between that utterance and its desired form in a way that indicated the changed articulation required for improvement, for example, in tongue position. A later application was made to improve the speech of children deaf from birth. I coauthored an article with Dan Kalikow in the *IEEE Transactions on Audio and Electroacoustics.*

A Psychology Laboratory

Programming the PDP-1 computer to provide a facile teaching machine also produced a general laboratory for experiments in perception, learning, and cognition. As far as audition is concerned, two reviewers wrote: "Swets, Green, and Winter (1961), in a highly innovative pioneering effort, were developing one of the first truly automated minicomputer labs for the study of auditory discrimination and auditory information processing, and which was to become the *prototype* [italics theirs] for almost all computer-automated auditory labs developed thereafter." Nice words that I redirect to BBN computer scientists Ed Fredkin and Bill Fletcher; Ed showed me in a few minutes how the computer could make sounds of choice and Bill stayed up all one night to program the computer to interact with experimental subjects.

No mean tricks, you will imagine, in the late 1950s. In those days, most computers accepted stacks of punched cards as input (from technicians who guarded the computers from the public) and printed stacks of paper output. The PDP-1 allowed users direct access to the computer and had what we called a "thin skin"—it would accept input, for example, from paper tape, typewriter, speech, or light pen and screen, and show comparable versatility of output. When BBN celebrated the arrival of the first production model of this machine, Fredkin arranged for it to cut its yellow ribbon.

Magnum Opus

Bob Taylor visited BBN upon taking a research-management position at NASA headquarters. He had learned of our signal detection work from a professor of his at the University of Texas, Lloyd Jeffress, a prominent psychologist at Acoustical Society meetings. Bob agreed to support a book that Dave Green and I would write, with NASA supporting half time for each of us for two years. (I spent mornings writing at home.) The result in 1966 was D. M. Green and J. A. Swets, *Signal Detection Theory and Psychophysics.* "Psychophysics"—the relation of stimulus to sensation—was the word Fechner coined to describe his work a century earlier. The book has done exceptionally well, and is now in its fourth printing, with approximately 5,000 citations. The current reprint by Peninsula Publishing has sold an average of sixty copies a year for last twenty years. (NASA could not support preparation of a commercially published book, but it could support a report to NASA that the authors might then arrange to publish as a book.)

Detection Research

Taylor introduced me to psychologists at NASA-Ames Research Center (California), who then supported my building a laboratory for signal detection research around a PDP-8 computer, which Dave Green and I kept busy for about five years. I chaired a symposium at Ames on "Applications of Research on Human Decisionmaking."

Alfred "Kris" Kistofferson, a friend at Michigan, moved from the University of Cincinnati to BBN during this time period. We worked together on detection studies of attention and provided the first chapter on attention in the *Annual Review of Psychology*. I published an earlier article on this topic in the *Psychological Bulletin*: "Central Processes in Auditory Frequency Analysis." The idea was that humans could tune in to different bands of auditory frequencies almost at will, sometimes to individual narrow bands, and sometimes to multiple bands.

Invited talks on detection research in symposia at Gothenberg, Paris (two), Moscow, Edinburgh, Stirling, St. Vincent, Washington, D.C., and Amherst, Massachusetts became book chapters. There were also meetings in Cassis and Berlin (two). More on these trips later. I reviewed in *Science* magazine an English translation of Gustav Fechner's (German) *Elements of Psychophysics* (1860), edited by E. G. Boring and former MIT colleague Davis Howes.

Professional Activities

The American Psychological Association (APA) and the American Association for the Advancement of Science (AAAS) elected me a fellow. The Acoustical Society of America (ASA) elected me a member of the executive council. I became more interested in vision than audition about then and did not continue actively with the Acoustical Society.

However, I continued passively and received in 2006 a fifty-year certificate from the society. And I wrote and presented orally the encomium for the award to Dave Green of the Society's gold medal.

Corporate Management

While serving as general manager, I had the opportunity to address the stockholders at BBN's annual meeting (BBN became a public company in 1962). I had heard for years that the stockholders saw no theme to BBN's work, and no coherent business. This was a genuine problem, because the company allowed staff members to work on almost any topic they chose, given that the individual or group could obtain financial support for it.

I described for the stockholders "The ABC's of BBN: From Acoustics to Behavioral Sciences to Computers," with the idea to show how these fields came to be the company's major areas and how they hung together. In short, the founding acousticians needed behavioral scientists (largely, psychologists) to work on speech and hearing, and on communication generally. And the psychologists interested in communication and information, were interested also in computers, particularly the new digital computers that were being developed. Another connection was that the psychologists worked on "human factors" and could see the need to make computers "user friendly."

There's not much to say about my performance and experiences as manager. I think I was more caretaker than innovator or builder. All went well until I realized I would rather do technical work. There was an element of selfishness to it; I preferred working for myself to working for 500 other people. The time I spent on technical matters while supposedly managing gives a clue. However, I note that the ARPANET—the first computer network and direct predecessor of the Internet—was built at BBN on my watch, and while I surely didn't make a direct contribution, neither did I get in the way. At the least, I was supportive.

Three other management positions came briefly to my attention. At one point, Leo Beranek suggested to BBN president Sam Labate that he (Leo) and I run the company in Sam's place; Sam didn't cotton to the idea. Former BBNer Tom Marill started the Computer Corporation of America and a few years later inquired if I might like to replace him as president, for its consolidation phase. Ed Fredkin suggested to Ken Olsen, president of the Digital Equipment Corporation, that DEC merge with BBN, and that I would possibly be manager of the BBN portion of the combined company. As I said, each possibility held the stage briefly.

A Berkeley Visit

While general manager, I tried to exercise some responsibility for the BBN offices outside of Cambridge by visiting them every two years or so, and made one swing to the offices in San Francisco and Los Angeles. I took the opportunity to spend an evening with Bob (Roger) and Esther Heyns in the chancellor's residence at Berkeley. On an after-dinner stroll through the central campus, Bob confided that he felt everyone depended on him—apparently many in a personal sense. This was easy for me to see because unrest on campus and in the community was near or at its peak (for example, the Peoples' Park demonstrations, if you remember them).

In wondering how Bob had arrived in his difficult position, I realized that I had broken with the Heyns-Swets tradition by following a path predominantly in science rather than administration. I offset contributions to society's current needs with the possibility of leaving some enduring knowledge. And I may have started to think more then about having it both ways—about using offshoots of fundamental science for societal purposes.

I had two more opportunities to visit the Heynses—first in their home on P street in Washington, D.C., when Bob was president of the American Council on Education; son Joe was with me. Bob told us how he had arranged a meeting at the White House with President Nixon's advisor, John Ehrlichman, in preparation for a meeting of a few university presidents with the president, hoping to improve the abysmal relations of the White House and academe. When he arrived, he was immediately sorry that he hadn't thought to take someone with him: Robert Haldeman was there and it was obvious that two versus one was not going to be any fun. The two advisors asked Heyns what his "guys" would tell Nixon to please him, and Bob said they would compliment the president on his China initiative. Erhlichman said he would call Heyns to give him a date, but the call never came: the Democratic offices at Watergate were broken into that night and the meeting was forgotten.

The second occasion to visit was in their home in Atherton, California, when Bob was president of the Hewlett Foundation and I was attending a meeting at the Center for Advanced Study in the Behavioral and Social Sciences in Palo Alto. Just pleasantries.

Tapes

During my time as BBN manager, federal authorities asked BBN to analyze three high-profile audio tapes of concern to the Department of Justice and congressional committees: tapes from Nixon's office recordings, the Kennedy assassination, and the Kent State shooting.

An advisory panel was formed under the chairmanship of BBN co-founder Dick Bolt to analyze the Watergate tapes. It included Acoustical Society friends Frank Cooper and Jim Flanagan, and met at BBN, where equipments including versatile computers were available. Focusing on the 18½-minute gap, the panel concluded that the erasure was deliberate, and that it could not recover the erased speech. The group met in a conference room adjacent to my office and I was able to facilitate the proceedings by ordering pizza brought in when they worked late.

Jim Barger was the lead BBN scientist analyzing the tape from the microphone left open on the Dallas motorcycle near the Kennedy shooting. He and his staff concluded that there might have been a second gunman, on the grassy knoll.

On a visit to Licklider in Washington, D.C., he took me to the assistant attorney general's office to pick up a tape recorded at Kent State to bring back to BBN for analysis. The tape was made by a student who had recorded from his windowsill in a dormitory room near the confrontation. I enlisted BBNer Chuck Dietrich to head the project and accompanied him to the university to look over the shooting scene and make some measurements. The tape did not provide relevant evidence, as to spoken commands to the National Guard or the order and identity of other acoustical events.

Diversions from Management

I chaired a working group for the National Research Council to recommend a new standard emergency evacuation signal (more later). With Lois Elliott, I edited the book *Psychology and the Handicapped Child* for the U.S. Office of Education, soliciting chapters from several prominent psychologists on how their subject areas and experiments could contribute to our knowledge of handicapped children and to their welfare. I spoke at a symposium in Berlin. I wrote a survey article for *Science* on the ROC in psychology, describing several new applications.

My invited talk at a conference at the University of Michigan Medical

School in 1970, on SDT methods for evaluating medical imaging techniques, was published as a book chapter, and turned out to anticipate the bulk of my subsequent research, through the year 2000—as described in the next chapter. The remainder of this chapter samples my nonmedical activities in the final phase of my BBN years.

Science Development Program

The SDP was led at its inception by Barger and me, then for ten years or so by Ray Nickerson, and by me again in my last ten or so years at the company. It was created to foster career development for technical staff. Its activities were aimed at developing the staff's capabilities, increasing BBN's stature and visibility, facilitating the development of new areas of research, and formalizing the opportunity for staff members to advance in the company along a technical career path. The SDP sponsors several technical seminar series and a guest lecturer series, gives financial awards for publications and patents, provides financial support for professional activities, for example, with national committees, professional societies, and journals, and supports visiting scientists.

I was able to host visiting scientists Charles Metz of the University of Chicago Medical School and Stephen Seltzer of the Harvard Medical School to pursue mutual interests in medical imaging. I also qualified for the sabbatical-leave program and was able to take three or four sabbaticals, in each case for writing a professional paper.

SDT and Nonmedical Diagnosis

"Vigilance"—military or industrial—is the practical detection problem; that is, in practice, unlike in laboratories, signals occur infrequently and not in defined intervals. A common finding was interpreted to mean that an observer's sensitivity declined sharply over time on watch, even within a half hour. However, performance was measured simply by the proportion of true-positive responses. ROC analysis, that is, keeping track of false positives as well, showed that these also declined sharply, thus indicating that the observer's decision threshold was becoming stricter over time. So, the behavioral effect was not a sensitivity issue, possibly due to fatigue or inattention, but rather an observer's free, conscious choice to tighten a decision threshold as he or she got a better estimate of the low signal probability. I discussed this problem in the afore-mentioned *Annual Review* chapter with Kristofferson and at a conference in St. Vincent, Italy; the latter discussion appeared as a book chapter.

"Nondestructive testing" is typified by finding cracks in airplane wings by means of ultrasound or eddy current. An analysis I made of Air Force data showed that individual observers varied widely, both in their accuracy and their decision thresholds. Accuracy varied across air-force bases from low to high, suggesting that procedures practiced at the top bases could be exported to those at bottom. The further suggestion is that supervisors use SDT techniques to get control of the decision threshold and decide on the optimal threshold for all observers. There is no point, after all, in having some observers take several planes out of service unnecessarily while others permit several dangerous planes to fly. I published the analysis in *Materials Evaluation,* but it failed to get much attention. That was too bad, because I slighted applications in medicine in order to proselytize in materials testing.

"System operators," such as airplane pilots, are often given warnings of danger. A common occurrence is that pilots come to respond slowly or not all to these warnings, and in some cases actually disable the warning devices. From their perspective, the devices have "cried wolf" too often to be credible. Moreover, the penalties of leaving the operational task to respond to warnings may be large. Indeed, not long ago, the Federal Aviation Administration ordered a shutdown of collision-warning devices on commercial airliners because of serious distractions they presented both to pilots and air-traffic controllers. This is a complex subject, but a general problem is that system designers set a low decision threshold for issuing a warning, in order that the system will rarely miss a truly dangerous condition. As a consequence that SDT can quantify, the probability of a false warning is then very high too, and the system breaks down. Colleagues Getty, Pickett, Gonthier, and I published an analysis of system warnings in the *Journal of Experimental Psychology: Applied.*[3]

"Aptitude testing" generally uses a correlation between test scores and the quality of the performance to be predicted to assess the validity of the predictive test. The correlation is based on continuous distributions of both the predictor and criterion variables. However, when the crite-

---

3. The article appeared in the first issue of the new journal, edited by Ray Nickerson of BBN.

rion performance has a two-valued outcome—for example, graduating or not, completing a self-paced course or not—SDT analysis is preferable to correlation coefficients. Lloyd Humphrey of the University of Illinois and I illustrated the point with his pilot-training data in the *Journal of Applied Psychology.*

"Disability determination," "survey research," and "weather prediction" are other diagnostic problems that I've studied with SDT methods, but we'll move on. Well, quickly I'll mention that I pursued the National Weather Service to substitute my methods for theirs but got nowhere. Several independent researchers in this field published articles to validate SDT methods and show their advantages.

Pattern Recognition

So far, we have considered signal "detection," or the task of distinguishing between just *two* alternatives: "Is a specified signal present or not," "Is signal *A* or signal *B* present?" BBNers Dave Getty, Ron Pickett, and I also studied the task of recognizing or identifying one of *many* signals, usually termed (pattern) "recognition." Here, the approach was to identify the common visual features of the patterns under consideration, measure the relative importance of each feature in distinguishing the patterns, and determine how to merge the features optimally into a recognition decision. We were supported in this work by the Office of Naval Research with the idea that the results could apply to recognizing sonar patterns. In the next chapter, I point out the relevance of this work to medical diagnosis.

Project Intelligence

Luis Alberto Machado was appointed Venezuelan Minister of State for the Development of Human Intelligence, holding the fervent belief that the intelligence of his country's children could and should be increased. His emissary, José Buscaglia, requested of Harvard University that it undertake a project to further this idea. The request was forwarded to Richard Herrnstein in the psychology department, who called me to see if BBN would define a project on which BBN and Harvard could collaborate. I passed the question on to Ray Nickerson and then Ray, Dick, José, and I traveled to Caracas to determine expectations there. After adjusting expectations to our comfort level, we framed a project with a goal to "improve the thinking skills" of Venezuelan children. We proceeded to design an experimental course and tests for seventh grade children in selected Venezuelan schools. I helped with direction of the project and traveled with others to the western, mountain town of Barquisimeto to get it started.

During a ceremonial program at Barquisimeto's teachers' college, we learned that there was local discontent with the idea of out-sourcing the project (supported by Petroleós de Venezuela) to the U.S. when a band of students stormed the speakers' platform and commandeered the microphone. They shortly left, but then stormed in again. José warned "This time they have guns" and I hit the deck. It turns out José was joking. And, indeed, things went well enough for us to declare the project a success and publish the results in the *American Psychologist*. Preparation of our curriculum was directed by BBN's Marilyn Adams; it was published and used in both Venezuela and the U.S. Marilyn recently sent me Venezuelan reports to indicate that there are now hundreds of schools, thousands of teachers, and some 200,000 students involved in offshoots of the various projects initiated by Minister Machado. Professor Dick Nesbitt of the University of Michigan recently contacted some of us who carried out the BBN project, with the idea of his replicating it.

Probabilistic Thinking Skills

A grant to BBN from the National Science Foundation supported a project I directed to design a technique and build a curriculum for teaching thinking skills in probabilistic reasoning under uncertainty. A computer-based course, with curriculum and software developed by coinvestigators Andee Rubin and Paul Horwitz, was pegged at the high-school level. The idea was to shift the focus of the typical course in statistics from statistical computation to statistical reasoning. We thought the resulting materials were appropriate to more advanced students as well and illustrated them at a conference at the Harvard Medical School, which was considering mathematical training for its students.

Evaluation of an NIH Division

The National Institutes of Health invited several research and consulting organizations to bid on a project to evaluate its Division of Research Resources. Dick Bolt and I assembled a blue-ribbon panel to consider the division's objectives and performance and BBN was awarded the project. Statistician Fred Mosteller served as chair of the panel and my cousin Jim Wyngaarden was a member. We made several visits to NIH and overall did a job that pleased the NIH administration and us.

Other Publications

I gave a talk on "the hill" to congressional staffers on "The Science of High-Stakes Decision Making in an Uncertain World" (sponsored by the Federation of Behavioral, Psychological, and Cognitive Sciences), which was printed as a separate report of a Public Policy Seminar series and reprinted in two books. Meanwhile, a pair of articles treated SDT's main concepts: one, the ROC accuracy measure and, two, mechanisms for choosing the best decision threshold in diagnostic settings—in *Science* and *American Psychologist,* respectively.

Another pair of articles was published in the *Psychological Bulletin.* One showed representative ROC data from a half-dozen areas in psychology and as many diagnostic fields; the other showed that common measures of accuracy not derived from SDT are based on assumptions that are inconsistent with those data and give invalid results.

I wrote an invited chapter for undergraduate students of cognitive science, and another on decision-making for adolescents. One of my favorite papers got lost as a book chapter in a volume edited by a friend, on mathematical models of attention. I mean that it would have received wider readership, and had some impact, as a journal article. It showed the application of models based on SDT to some new sets of data that had gained wide attention.

In 1996, some of my published articles were collected as a book: *Signal Detection Theory and ROC Analysis in Psychology and Diagnostics.* Three sections, with informative introductions, contained twelve chapters that reproduced the basic theory, methods, and data and a range of applications. I was disappointed by the rather low level of interest— what I think of as the convenience of having several reference articles together and integrated, others may have thought of as paying for articles that one can get for free.

More Professional Activities

Here is a list of a few of the outside professional activities that kept me meeting people and addressing new problems:

Science Advisory Board, Navy Personnel Research and Development Center, San Diego CA

Panel on "Youth at Risk," MacArthur Foundation

Forum on Research Management of the Federation of Behavioral, Psychological, and Cognitive Sciences

Senior Consultant, Federal Inter-Agency Coordinating Committee on the Human Brain Project

Council, American Association for the Advancement of Science

Executive Committee, International Society for Psychophysics

Presidential Faculty Fellows Panel, National Science Foundation

Member of the Board, German-American Research Foundation

Question of Moving

I had a few chances to consider professorships. They were usually single telephone conversations with people I knew, but sometimes included visits and interviews. I have no notes, but remember Columbia, Indiana, Vanderbilt, Florida, New Mexico, Northwestern, McMaster, Irvine, Dartmouth, Michigan—all delightful places, but I was having fun at BBN and my family was settling into the Boston-Cambridge area.

Actually, Leo Beranek may have cut off a possible move to Michigan by a tactic of the sort he invented as needed. I was planning to interview at Michigan during a meeting in Ann Arbor of the Acoustical Society; Leo apparently got wind of this plan and suggested that he and I share a room at the Michigan Union during the meeting. My parents came to see me and Leo took us out to dinner. My mother told me afterward that she, of course, was hoping that I would be able to move my family back to Michigan, but that Leo was such a fine gentleman that she could understand my wanting to stay at BBN.

Three friends influential at their universities—Cincinnati, Stanford, and Syracuse, respectively—asked me if I were willing to be nominated for the presidencies of those institutions. I remember thinking I'd do it if I could have son Steve as vice president for external affairs and son Joe as vice president for internal affairs. (What's the word for "extreme partiality"?)

I thought that BBN had a pretty good psychology department. Even a coloration I liked, with Michigan Ph.D.'s Dick Pew, Allan Collins, Sanford Fidell, Glenn Jones, Alfred Kristofferson, Ed Smith, and Walter Reitman. (The word is "chauvinism.")

6   ROC and Medicine

Medical Imaging—Accuracy

As I gave up management at BBN to return to research, a representative of the National Cancer Institute (NCI), Judith Prewitt, came calling. She had heard my talk in Ann Arbor on SDT and medical imaging and she said that the NCI wanted me to apply SDT to evaluate the accuracy of the new Computer-Assisted Tomograph (then known as the "CAT scanner") and also the relative accuracy of three forms of mammography, and to set forth a protocol that would be a standard for evaluating medical-imaging techniques in general. I enlisted BBNer Ronald Pickett and convinced a BBN manager to hire psychologist David Getty from Brown University—and we submitted a proposal to follow the NCI's request. Ron had written a book on human factors in medicine and Dave knew a lot about human perception and computers; both were savvy statisticians. (After our proposal was submitted, it was determined that a noncompetitive, "sole-source," contract award would not be permitted and we reworked our proposal to win a competition.)

Computer Tomography

We were to compare the accuracy of computed tomography (CT) scans and radionuclide (RN) scans in detecting and diagnosing brain lesions. We obtained several hundred images of both kinds from the five medical centers that had acquired CT scanners at that early date and had participated in a collaborative study sponsored by the NCI. We enlisted six expert radiologists for each device to come to BBN to read the images under controlled conditions, using response forms that we had constructed. Each radiologist spent six days in our lab over a period of six months, reading the type of image in which they specialized. Images of both types were taken on each patient in the study. The response form elicited information to construct an ROC, as well as judgments about location and type of lesion. Dave Getty arranged probably the first computer display of several (eight) CT slices simultaneously on a single computer screen.

Our study found the CT technique to be clearly superior to the RN technique. The results were published in *Science,* and hence assured a broad audience, in 1979. Son Joe was one of seven coauthors of that article, having signed on as research assistant at BBN for two years between college and law school. He administered the reading test for each radiologist visit. His main technical contribution was to adapt the ROC to three categories of response—*yes, no,* or *doubtful*—as described in an article that he and I coauthored. At the same time (1979), I published a review article in *Investigative Radiology,* extending SDT to a variety of questions asked in medical imaging. James Adelstein, Dean for Academic Programs, hosted me for a grand rounds talk at the Harvard Medical School.

I've been noting right along my articles that appeared in *Science* magazine and have just reached the sixth and final one; I'm proud of this collection, and suspect that six is near the record for this general science magazine.[1]

Mammography

We were also to evaluate three types of mammography: industrial film, Lo-Dose film, and Xerography. (The last-named type was based on the

---

1. The *Science* articles are:
   Is there a sensory threshold? (1961)
   Information retrieval systems (1963)
   Computer-aided instruction (1965)
   The relative operating characteristic in psychology (1973)
   Assessment of diagnostic techniques (1979)
   Measuring the accuracy of diagnostic systems (1988)

Xerox process and gave a positive image as distinguished from the negative films.) We received images from a collaborative study supported by the NCI and found they were collected to study variables other than accuracy, so that we could not make a reliable, comparative ROC analysis. We could, however, use readings of the images to develop several new statistical techniques for assessing various aspects of imaging studies, as part of a general protocol for imaging studies.

Spreading the Word

For our NCI study, we enlisted an advisory panel of experts in medical imaging and statistics. Not fully anticipated was the result that each of them would become expert in the application of SDT to imaging techniques and go on to popularize this application in the medical field. James Adelstein and Barbara McNeil of the Harvard Medical School wrote an influential tutorial article in the *New England Journal of Medicine*. Barbara wrote several other articles as well, notably on ROC statistics. Lee Lusted of the University of Chicago had first presented a discussion of SDT in a 1968 book on medical decision-making and went on to feature the ROC in a new journal he edited on *Medical Decision Making*. Charles Metz, also of the University of Chicago Medical School, wrote tutorial articles, including one in *Seminars in Nuclear Medicine* that has received more than a thousand citations. Charles developed statistical computer programs for fitting ROC data that became international standards; approximately 15,000 thousand investigators requested and received free copies of his software. Harold Kundel of the University of Pennsylvania published prolifically in this area—including, as lead author, a comprehensive report by the International Commission on Radiological Units. J. E. K. Smith, a classmate and friend of mine in the University of Michigan's psychology department, and at the time of our study a professor there, made contributions to sophisticated statistical methods.

Collaborations

Close collaborations developed between Barbara, Charles, and the BBN staff. Much of the time we met weekly at BBN. Charles came to Cambridge several times a year for a week (and often spent an evening with Mickey and me). Steven Seltzer of Harvard Medical School and Carl D'Orsi of the University of Massachusetts Medical School joined the team, and spent sabbatical and visiting-scientist time at BBN. A half dozen or so joint contracts or grants supported us for twenty-five years—sometimes with BBN, sometimes with a medical school, as the prime contractor. I became a Lecturer in Preventive Medicine and Clinical Epidemiology at Harvard Medical School in 1984, and later moved to the Department of Health Care Policy when it was set up with Barbara as chair.

Steven became chair of the Brigham and Womens' Hospital's radiology department and arranged appointments there for Ron, Dave, and me as senior research associates; in later years we met weekly there. Carl arranged for me to give a grand rounds talk at the University of Massachusetts medical school. I was a member of a committee chaired by Fred Mosteller to suggest enhancements of the curriculum in quantitative sciences in Harvard's medical area. I arranged a symposium at a Denver meeting of the American Association for the Advancement of Science, with a slate consisting of Barbara McNeil, Charles Metz, Harvey Fineberg (Harvard), and Emmett Keeler (Rand).

Protocol / Book

The protocol, or set of standard methods, desired by the NCI was published as a book by Academic Press (1982), authored by J. A. Swets and R. M. Pickett: *Evaluation of Diagnostic Systems: Methods from Signal Detection Theory.*

Part I on Quantitative Methods presents chapters on:
Fundamentals of accuracy analysis
Extensions of accuracy analysis
Statistical design of a performance test
Statistical treatment of accuracy results
Forms of efficacy analysis

Part II on Experimental Methods covers:
Elements of study design
Procedure of a performance test
Drawing the original case sample
Selection of test cases
Selection of test readers

Part III contains an illustrative evaluation of imaging systems, based on our mammography study. As mentioned, the mammography materials available to us did not support a comparative accuracy study, so we designated the three types of mammography as X, Y, and Z. Several useful appendices were also included.

Evaluation then Enhancement

From this focus on *evaluation* of imaging techniques, we shifted our attention to the *enhancement* of techniques, Without altering image quality, we undertook to increase the radiologist's perceptual and decision-making skills through development of computer-based aids that support and refine their judgment of the images. We studied, and developed various supportive tools for various imaging techniques, including mammography, staging of prostate cancer by magnetic resonance imaging (MRI), cataract photography, and MRI of liver lesions.

Feature-Based Diagnosis

The usual approach to image reading is to treat the visual-assessment process in a global, holistic, manner at first, and then proceed to particulars. Our approach was to analyze the image in its component parts, and to treat the parts separately first, and then together, in a quantitative way. We termed this latter approach a *feature-based* approach.

Following on the Navy-supported work mentioned in chapter 5, we determined through perceptual studies and statistical analysis which visual features are important to a diagnosis for a given type of image and type of disease. We further determined how important these features are relative to one another, and developed computer programs to merge a reader's ratings of these features for a given case into the basis for a diagnostic decision. Picture a radiologist keying into a computer a rating of each of the total list of features, usually on a ten-point scale, and receiving from the computer a probability that is the best estimate of the existence of the abnormality in question. The radiologist can then use that probability in coming to a final decision.

For mammography, the important features of a "mass" in the image were found to include its locus, size, shape, density, roughness of border—thirteen features in all. The diagnosis of "clustered calcifications" in a mammogram depends on characteristics of the granular elements, such as branching, number in a cluster, size, shape, smoothness, and uniformity—eleven features in all. "Secondary signs" include nipple or skin retraction, skin thickening, enlarged prominent duct, and a feature called architectural distortion. It was not a surprise, given the technique's long history, that the set of features we determined served largely to confirm the features typically used by mammography specialists, rather than to reveal any novel features. We found, however, that use of these features with ratings and computer estimate served consistently to bring the performance of general, community-based radiologists up to the level of specialists. At an appropriate decision threshold, we estimated that generalists using the feature- and computer-based system would find thirteen more cancers in one hundred cases of malignancy.

In another breast-imaging study, we determined by statistical analysis the relevant features of a largely untried technique based on light scanning, called "diaphanography." For this imagery, nine new features were identified and gave a substantial increase in accuracy over unaided human readers.

For prostate-cancer staging, the feature-analytic approach again produced certain features that the radiologists had not been considering. Use of the diagnostic aids in laboratory studies led to a true-positive probability fifteen points higher than that obtained without the aids, leading to fifteen more cancers found in a set of one hundred malignancies. Positive results, revealing novel features, were also obtained in the diagnosis of visual cataracts and liver disease.

The computer can merge feature ratings across imaging techniques—or more generally, across quantitative tests or demographic variables —as well as across visual features within an imaging technique. In our examination of prostate cancer, considering *age* alone gave an accuracy of .56 (on a .50 to 1.00 scale); age combined with *prostate specific androgen (PSA)* gave .74; those two variables plus the *biopsy Gleason score* yielded .81; and those three variables plus *magnetic resonance imaging (MRI)* gave .88. Each additional variable that is considered leads to several more cancers found, or, for a more conservative threshold, several more benign cases identified as such.

Other Benefits

We foresaw benefits of feature analysis in four other respects. One is in having a *standardized language*. There has been an increasing national clamor among physicians and surgeons for standardization of radiological reports of all sorts. Many pointed to mammography reports as being most in need of a standardization upgrade. (The critics have said that the flower of the Radiological Society is the hedge.) Our feature set was a major input to the standard lexicon for mammography developed by the American College of Radiology. This lexicon was finalized by a committee of the ACR that was cochaired by two of our collaborators: Carl D'Orsi of the University of Massachusetts Medical School, and Daniel Kopans of the Harvard Medical School.

Second, working with perceptual features can facilitate the *training of radiologists*, for example, by automatically tailoring a computer-based instruction program to the individual's needs. Third, recording feature ratings allows facile *reconciliation of multiple opinions*, to increase efficiency of a department's quality assurance programs.

Fourth, the feature ratings and probability judgment for a case can provide the ingredients of an *automated, standardized, prose report* to the referring physician and to the department's database. This time-saver may compensate the radiologist for time spent in rating features. We would add to an image-reading system the computer's ability to recognize spoken feature ratings, so the radiologist need not look away from the images being read. Unfortunately, time ran out before our research team could build the envisioned system and demonstrate its value. But it will happen—in about ten years if our experience holds true.

Decision Threshold

Turning from accuracy to the other component of ROC analysis, namely, the decision threshold, I found that the best illustrations of the value of this analysis come from failures to apply it—such as for tests that detect the human immunodeficiency virus (HIV), the cause of AIDS. As I wrote in a *Scientific American* article in 2000, the FDA approved three HIV tests, aimed at a specific population, that differed significantly both in their accuracies and decision thresholds. Apparently, thought was not given to using just the most accurate test and then setting the decision threshold at the single most appropriate level.

What's more, the thresholds originally set to distinguish clean from tainted blood were left unchanged when the tests were enlisted to identify people infected with the virus. Now, throwing out a pint of uncontaminated blood because of a false-positive diagnosis is a cheap mistake; sending an alarmed, uninfected person for further HIV testing is not. It makes sense to raise the decision threshold in going from blood to people, to reflect the higher cost of false-positive decisions.

The original thresholds were applied to low-risk blood donors, high-risk donors, military recruits, and methadone-clinic visitors—groups whose infection rates vary over an enormous range. An ROC cost-benefit analysis would lead to a lower threshold for high-risk groups than for low—if up to half of the sample is infected (an estimated 45,000 of 100,000 for methadone-clinic visitors), a low threshold should be used to issue many positive decisions. Conversely, conservatism makes sense when almost no one in the test group (an estimated 30 per 100,000 for low-risk blood donors) is truly infected.

The HIV problem is complicated by the procedure of using a relatively inexpensive screening test followed by a more accurate, more expensive follow-up test. I read of one clinic that set a threshold for each individual on the second test—higher or lower—depending on the degree of positivity of the outcome of that individual's first test, but such sophistication is not widely shared.

Lately, with the advent of more accurate tests and, especially, better therapies, the emphasis has shifted from whom to call positive to whom to test. The costs and benefits now indicate that almost every adult should be screened. It pays more to identify diseased people when the decisions are surer and when something can be done to help them.

One reads often of concerns that screening for prostate cancer calls too many men positive and subjects them to further testing, when in fact a large share of them don't have the disease. This cancer is a slow-growing disease, so that doing nothing, or "watchful waiting," may often be appropriate. However, one reads little or nothing of the threshold issue. For years, the policy for many physicians has been to do further testing (biopsy) if the test value of the prostate-specific antigen (PSA) is four or higher. Setting the threshold at five or six might be preferable. Again, one could raise the threshold value for the biopsy result (Gleason score), from the customary six to seven or eight.

Admittedly, not all threshold issues are tight logic and numbers. Mammograms, for example, are characteristically read very leniently. This approach fits the fact that patients who receive a negative biopsy result are more inclined to be grateful to the mammographer for establishing the absence of disease than critical of a mammogram reading that erroneously led to concern and a biopsy.

7   Affairs of the Profession

Two Awards

The Society of Experimental Psychology (SEP) was founded in 1938 to hold an annual meeting to discuss scientific psychology, and the society came to serve the purpose also of honoring its members (membership is by invitation and limited). Dave Green and I were jointly awarded the Howard Crosby Warren Medal of the Society in 1985. The citation read:

> For their considerable contributions
> to signal detection theory and to auditory psychophysics.
> Their application of decision theory to many areas
> of experimental psychology has had great theoretical
> and practical impact, as have their
> experimental and theoretical studies of audition.

(Dave observed, because I studied decisions in psychology and practical settings and he studied audition, that the citation gave us each every other line.)

I attended the annual meetings of the SEP regularly for fifteen years or so and once hosted the meeting at BBN as society chair. SEP was dominated for decades by East coast members in sensory, physiological, and learning psychology, but has evolved to reflect current trends in the field; especially cognitive psychology, geographical spread, and gender parity.

Dave and I decided to use the money that came with the medal to set up a fund to honor Spike Tanner, by then deceased. Al Cain, department chair at Michigan, helped contact alumni and faculty who would be interested, and the fund grew to support awards each year to three undergraduates. The Tanner Awards help support research and provide funds to present papers at national meetings.

In 1990, the American Psychological Association (APA) presented me its Distinguished Scientific Contribution Award. (Dave had received this award earlier.) The citation read:

> For his pioneering work on the theory of signal detection and its application to psychophysics, work that caused a paradigm shift in sensory psychology in which the idea of a discrete threshold was replaced with that of a continuously-variable detection process. For his role in establishing clearly the importance of decision criterion as well as acuity as a determinant of performance in any discrimination task. For a steady stream of important theoretical and empirical papers using signal detection theory to further our understanding of human perception and cognition, and demonstrating its applicability to the evaluation of diagnostic systems in a variety of domains including weather forecasting, materials testing, information retrieval, polygraph lie detection, aptitude testing, and medical decision making.

I surely appreciate Ray Nickerson's proposing me for this award and Dick Pew's traveling to a San Francisco APA meeting to introduce me for the talk I gave in connection with accepting it.

Both awards for scientific accomplishments were made after I had left science for management, and, hence, after my scientific peers might have been expected to give me up for lost. It was bad enough from their perspective that I had earlier left academe for industry. ("Industry" puts it in the least favorable light; as mentioned earlier, BBN was thought by some to be Cambridge's third university, and was at least a "think-tank.") However, whether I could or would redeem myself was an open question when I returned to research, and I'm surely pleased that I did to the extent of these two deeply treasured awards.

Two Academies

I was elected to the National Academy of Sciences (NAS) in 1990 and the American Academy of Arts & Sciences (AAAS) in 1993.

The NAS was established in 1863 by a congressional act signed by Abraham Lincoln. It was dedicated to the advancement of science and the application of science to promote the general welfare. It acts as advisor to the government upon request. It and its sister institutions—the

National Academy of Engineering and the Institute of Medicine—conduct scientific studies (not original research) through their working arm, the National Research Council (NRC).

The NAS has about 2,000 elected members, including about 70 psychologists. Some 6,000 individuals participate in the NRC's 600 or so studies under way. President Obama spoke at the NAS annual meeting, after his "first 100 days," on April 27, 2009.

NAS president Frank Press read this citation at the annual meeting when I was elected:

> Swets has made a significant impact on psychophysics, the study of the relation between stimuli and human responses. By applying the theory of signal detection, he created a new paradigm for the study of human sensory systems.

I cherish the memories of a party given for me by my colleague Dick and Sue Pew to celebrate the election. At this point in our careers, I was a member of the BBN Department of Experimental Psychology headed by Dick (or maybe by then it was the Cognitive Science and Systems Department).

The AAAS was founded by the Massachusetts Legislature in 1780, led by John Adams and John Hancock, to provide thoughtful analysis of issues critical to the establishment of the republic. Located in Cambridge, Massachusetts, it has provided a forum over the years for 11,000 men and women elected to membership—scholars, members of the learned professions, government, and business leaders. Like the NAS, it has the dual function of electing members of exceptional achievement and conducting programs, projects, and studies of issues of the day—in the case of AAAS, issues as broad as society.

When I was elected in 1993, then-AAAS-President Leo Beranek recognized the new fellows individually at the annual membership ceremony and was highly pleased to do so for someone he had hired at BBN.

NAS Activities

Attending the annual meetings of the NAS has been very rewarding, as has participating in its affairs, both on the levels of the Psychology Section and the Academy at large. At the section level, I was chair for three years and then liaison to the NRC. My time as chair of the Psychology Section was recognized by the succeeding chair John Anderson in his first letter to the section members as follows (if you will permit me):

> Let me begin this mailing by thanking John Swets, and on behalf of the membership of the Section, for his outstanding leadership for the last three years. His qui-

et, yet extremely effective style helped the Section emerge from the turmoil associated with divergent interests caused by disparate areas of coverage to the present state of cooperation and respect. He then facilitated the division of the section that helped NAS recognize the immense growth of the neurosciences, and he made the change proceed smoothly and without controversy. His will be a hard act to follow. For my part I will try to continue the obviously effective style and policies of my predecessor. Fortunately, he has agreed to tutor me in how this is done. As can be observed, I am following the format of his past letters.[1]

For the Academy I served variously as member of the nominating committee, NRC's Board of Governors, and president's committee on educational reform, and I carried out an interesting assignment for President Press:

The president asked me to try to resolve some issues raised in the context of the Troland Award, an award for which the recipient was selected by a committee of the Psychology Section. It had been set up in 1984, with a cash prize (now $50,000) to help support an individual under 40 whose work reflected Leonard T. Troland's interests in "experimental psychology given quantitative treatment and seeking physiological explanation." The wording of the nature of the work that was eligible for the award was settled on, with great care for nuances and amid strong opinions, by lions of psychology Leo Hurwich, Bill Estes, and Duncan Luce. In 1992, Nobelist Herb Simon, a member of another section, noticed that the Troland funds had grown to permit two annual awards each year and he wished to broaden the nature of the eligible quantitative work to include formal treatments such as explicit algorithms (for example, computer modeling) and symbolic logics of various types.

Simon's letter to Frank Press was passed on to me; I carried on an e-mail correspondence for a couple of months with the four principals named above, and we hit upon a new statement of eligible work that was accepted by all. We extended the scope of quantitative work as Herb suggested and asked committees to attempt to balance the two annual awards between quantitative and physiological work. Ken Fulton, executive director of NAS, who was acquainted with the award definition's vibrant history, said he thought I should be dispatched to the Middle East. I served on the Troland committee three or four times, once as chair. That year (still with one award), I introduced reward recipient Martha Farah to Academy members at its annual meeting.

---

1. This may be as good a time as any to mention that I don't congratulate myself or repeat others' favorable comments on me outside of this memoir.

National Research Council

In my early professional years, I served on various working groups of the NRC established by two standing committees—on hearing and bioacoustics (CHABA) and on vision (COV). One that stands out was a working group I chaired to design a new standard emergency evacuation signal.

Evacuation Signal

The expectation was that the working group would design a distinctive acoustic signal that would be capable of permeating several different acoustic noise environments, in settings such as malls, factories, and so on. The group instead proposed a distinctive *temporal* signal that could be used with any type of acoustic signal—bell, horn, whatever. Specifically proposed was a repetitive signal of two short pulses followed by a longer pulse (dot-dot-dash). This recommendation, the last I heard, was accepted by international standards organizations but is yet to be put into practice. The working group's final report is known as the NRC's shortest, namely, one page in the *Journal of the Acoustical Society of America*. Four BBNers served on the eight-member group, including Dave Green, Karl Kryter, Ted Schultz, and me.

Extraordinary Training Techniques

"Be all that you can be," the well-known slogan of the U.S. Army a few years back, was advanced by General Maxwell Thurman, then in charge of recruitment. Later, he was head of the Army training command that included the Army Research Institute (ARI) for behavioral-science research. In supporting the training involved, the general became interested in several extraordinary techniques for enhancing human performance. These included techniques for accelerating learning, learning during sleep, altering mental states, managing behavior under stress, influencing other people by programming them neuro-linguistically, split-brain learning, biofeedback, and paranormal techniques for viewing remote sites and influencing the operation of distant machines. The ARI desired to have this set of unconventional techniques evaluated as a class, by the NRC, rather than to succumb to the general's desire to fund several individual projects. I was enlisted as chair of the NRC committee, but I think (except for a misleading title) that a *New York Times* account summarizes the results of the committee's efforts better than I can:

ARMY'S LEARNING PANEL URGES OFFBEAT STUDIES
By Warren E. Leary, Special to the *New York Times*
Published December, 1987

There is little or no evidence that unconventional learning techniques will help the Army produce better soldiers, a National Research Council committee said today. But the panel said some methods deserved further study.

The panel studied a variety of techniques, ranging from trying to teach different things to different sides of the brain, to using extrasensory perception. But it said most of the unconventional learning and motivational techniques it examined lacked adequate evidence to support assumptions of effectiveness.

"Often, the only evidence supporting claims of many performance-enhancement techniques are testimonials from satisfied users, which tend to be unreliable," said Dr. John Swets, chairman of the panel, at a news briefing.

"To be sure, a lack of scientific evidence for a technique does not necessarily mean that it doesn't work," he said. "It does mean that the Army should test the technique in a properly controlled setting before purchasing it for use by soldiers." Dr. Swets is chief scientist at Bolt Beranek & Newman, a Cambridge, Mass. research and consulting concern.

The 14-member committee of psychologists, educators, and training specialists conducted the three-year study at the request of the Army Research Institute. The study cost $425,000. Despite the lack of evidence for certain methods, Dr. Swets said, it still made sense for the Army to be interested in performance enhancement because the services must train thousands of recruits each year in skills, including operating sophisticated equipment.

The research council, the operating arm of the National Academy of Sciences and Engineering [sic], cited some techniques that appeared to be useful and deserve further study,

For example, it said some aspects of learning while asleep deserve more attention. Material presented to people in lighter stages of sleep, but not deep sleep, seemed to improve their ability to learn or recall the material, the panel said.

Dr. Robert Bjork of the University of California, Los Angeles, another panelist, said sleep learning might be useful in teaching simple elements of foreign languages or for learning codes.

The panel also said mental practice, the process of watching experts perform a task and mentally repeating their moves, "is effective in enhancing the performance of motor skills," especially those that are mentally challenging.

One technique that showed no promise as yet was learning by targeting certain information to specific hemispheres of the brain, or seeking to integrate activities from both sides of the brain, the panel said. A substantial body of research points to differences in how the two hemispheres of the brain process information, with the left side being more involved in speech and language and the right concentrating on visual and spatial information.

This type of brain targeting should not be considered further by the Army unless some valid evidence becomes available, the panel concluded.

Dr. Ray Hyman, a panelist from the University of Oregon in Eugene, said the committee found no evidence of the existence or usefulness of elements of parapsychology, including ESP, telepathy of thought projection, and mind-over-matter psychokinesis.

"Even when you look at the best work in parapsychology, it is flawed, even by its own standards," Dr. Hyman said. "We found that many of the studies cited in this field have inadequate controls, lack documentation or make the wrong use of statistics in reaching their conclusions."

The panel said there was no scientific justification for the claims of parapsychology and concluded that the Army need not research these phenomena further.

Biofeedback, a technique that allows a person to monitor his or her physiological state and correlate it with learning and other activities, seemed to help reduce muscle tension, the committee said. The studies, however, do not correlate this tension relief with reduced emotional and mental stress, as has been contended by proponents.

Robert Bjork, a committee member mentioned above, helped me considerably with my duties as chair of the committee, so that I came to think of him as the committee's unofficial vice chair. We became firm friends and his name will enter this story again, here and later. NAS study director Dan Druckman made contributions across the range of topics and gave very competent logistic support.

Bjork, Druckman, ARI director Ed Johnson, and I were helicoptered to General Thurman's headquarters at Fort Monroe, Virginia, to make the committee's report to him. A meeting scheduled for forty-five minutes lasted almost four hours. In accepting the generally negative report, the general said that he had been listening to his gurus of the time and he was wrong. He was intensely interested in our review of how mainstream psychology could help with the problems he faced, and the committee was rechartered to pursue those leads. It proceeded through three more phases, the first two skillfully chaired by Bjork and the third by Jerome Singer, with all three ably supported by Druckman. At General Thurman's invitation, I gave an after-dinner talk to a group of general officers meeting at Fort Leavenworth.[2]

The book that served as the first-phase committee report—*Enhancing Human Performance: Issues, Theories, and Techniques*—was general-

---

2. General Thurman became commander of the Army's Southern Command in 1989, when he attempted to oust General Manuel Noriega from control in Panama. Thurman's unconventional approach then was to try to drive Noriega from his sanctuary with constant loud music.

ly well received (outside of parapsychology). We appreciated a review by Philip Morrison in *Scientific American*. His summary: "Among the most difficult lessons to learn in science is how not to deceive yourself. This patient and judicious overview offers genuine help." Bob Bjork and I reviewed committee work and experiences in an article in the new journal *Psychological Science*, which contained a handsome color photo of the committee taken on the beach during a San Diego meeting.

However, lest my account make the effort seem more staid than it was, I quote from Dan Druckman: "[The committee's report was] one of the most unusual books ever published by academic psychologists. Referred to within the Academy as the 'spoon-bending' committee, our group took on the vested interests surrounding a variety of exotic techniques with extraordinary claims of effectiveness, including topics that any respectable academic would not touch with a ten-foot pole, namely, extra-sensory perception and neuro-linguistic programming!"[3]

Polygraph Lie Detection

Can liars be caught—specifically, by measuring physiological processes? Recently, I served on an NRC committee to evaluate the accuracy of the polygraph in lie detection. This is a problem begging for signal detection theory: one wants to know the polygraph's accuracy in ROC terms and to observe the different balances of true positives and false positives that are attainable with that accuracy.

The committee was set up in response to a request by the Department of Energy, which was concerned by security infractions, usually spying, in its laboratories at Los Alamos. A central characteristic of the DOE's application of the polygraph is that DOE proposes to screen thousands of employees, only a few of whom—in single digits—are expected to be guilty. We say there is a low prior probability of the event in question, or a low "base rate." This situation is reminiscent of the information-retrieval problem mentioned in chapter 5: a file of items, say in a conventional library, may be expected to contain only a few items relevant to a

---

3. A posting by the American Association for the Advancement of Science on its web page (November 9, 2009) reports on the new movie *The Men Who Stare at Goats,* with George Clooney in the lead role. The movie portrays the Army's interest in the paranormal during the 1980s and the posting refers to the NRC's report as recommending that the Army abandon its research on the subject. (My own bet is that the Army's interest continues.)

specific query at hand. The killer in this situation is that obtaining a large share of the relevant items (true positives) brings along—in the mixture—an unmanageable number of irrelevant items (false positives). So we speak of the "curse of the low base rate." How many innocent people are the DOE willing to call guilty for each guilty person it detects?

The committee's final report gave this example: Assume a very generous ROC accuracy of 0.90 and a population of 10,000 examinees containing 10 spies. If one wants to catch 8 of the 10 spies, on average, a low decision threshold must be set, such that the polygraph exam will call about 1,600 innocent people spies (mixed with the 8). If now the decision threshold is raised, in order to reduce the number of false positives, say, to about 40, then only 2 of the 10 spies will be called spies (mixed with the 40) and 8 spies will be free to cause further damage. But the DOE doesn't get it. An April 30, 2007 memo notified Los Alamos employees that polygraph tests of 8,000 employees were to be conducted. Meanwhile, the employees understand the false-positive problem and realize how high the chances are of being falsely accused. We can imagine the effect on morale.

The Commission on Behavioral and Social Sciences and Education

The NRC studies just reviewed were conducted under the auspices of CBASSE, one of a half dozen commissions in the NRC (now called "divisions" rather than "commissions"). I was a member of CBASSE for five years, then its chair for three years. My wonderfully capable and personable associates were division directors Suzanne Woolsey and Barbara Torrey, and department heads Alexandra Wigdor and Christine Hertel.

The eighteen commissioners functioned as an advisory and approval board; its projects were implemented by permanent staff. The focus, of both the commission and the division, has been on five broad areas: human performance, children and families, population issues, education reform, and statistical methods and information.

Workplace Safety

In the spring of 1998, the National Institute for Occupational Safety and Health sought congressional approval to implement an ergonomic standard for the workplace—essentially a regulation that would require businesses to take various steps to reduce the number of workplace injuries. The standard was to become effective in the fall of that year. Republicans in the House would liked to have killed the bill, to spare small businesses the expense, but did not have the votes, and so sought to delay it by calling for a study by the NRC of the "science" behind the standard.

The House committee that oversaw the budget of the National Institutes of Health instructed the NIH to sponsor such an NRC study. The NRC's Division of Behavioral and Social Sciences and Education (DBASSE) proposed a two-year study to answer seven questions posed by the House committee.

At this point, the Democratic presidential administration urged the NIH director, who served at the president's discretion, to arrange instead a six-month study that would not cause delay in implementation. DBASSE politely declined to conduct a study it could not defend. But the NIH director needed more help than that from the NRC and called for a meeting in his office to be attended by the NRC chairman (who was also the president of the National Academy of Sciences), no doubt having in mind that the NIH accounted for a substantial share of the NRC budget. However, the NRC chairman was scheduled to be out of the country during the period in which the proposed NIH meeting could be held, and so a substitute was needed for him..

But who to send? NRC officials called me, as an NAS member and former chair of the commission that oversaw DBASSE, to see if I would go —maybe "run an errand" for them is how they put it. I agreed, with the proviso that Dick Pew of BBN would accompany me; whereas I couldn't spell "workplace safety," Dick could, and he had a long history with NRC studies. He and I went to NIH with two scientific officers of the NRC (to find, incidentally, that the NIH director had called in for the discussion six specialists in workplace safety presently conducting NIH-sponsored research). I was supposed to discuss the constraints on NRC studies, such as a fairly lengthy review process for a study report, but the NIH director waved several reports of NRC studies in which he had participated, a couple of which he had chaired, to shorten that discussion.

Fortunately, the two sides hit upon an amicable agreement, that the NRC would conduct a six-month study—to "address," rather than "answer," the seven questions of the House committee—by means of a "workshop," essentially a dozen or so talks—rather than a twelve-or-so-member committee meeting five or six times to draw unanimous conclusions. Time was saved partly by the fact that the NRC report-review process is less rigorous for workshops than for full-blown studies. Dick chaired the steering committee for the workshop. Its report did not claim that ergonomic problems occurred only in the workplace, but strongly supported the position that it was a major source of such injuries.

I learned from Dick recently that the ergonomic standard was not implemented that year, because Congress was not satisfied that the scientific case had been "proved," and that a second study was performed by the NRC, a two-year study of the sort originally requested. A final ergonomic standard became effective when the latter study concluded.

Institute of Medicine

I served on two committees of the IOM, neither of which did a very good job, in my opinion. One was charged "to identify promising areas of social science and behavioral research that could improve the public's health," specifically, to identify promising "intervention strategies," programs that would improve health through affecting behavior. The committee treated the charge in very general terms, giving properties of successful interventions, but nary a single concrete example of a successful intervention. I thought it should give several, as did the report reviewers and the foundation that supported the study. There were a few other examples of my anticipating the reviewers' criticisms.

The second IOM committee was to advise the Social Security Administration as it sought to design a new decision process for the determination of disability. The SSA thought it could try a new process, without first evaluating the current process against measurable criteria in order to have a baseline performance and some idea of problems in the current system. The committee strongly recommended "that before making the changes in the current decision process, SSA should establish evaluative criteria for measuring the performance of the decision process, conduct research studies and analyses to determine how the current processes work relative to these pre-established criteria, and then evaluate the extent to which change would lead to improvement."

This advice seems like common sense, but the SSA decided that following it would be too difficult, and that the SSA would give up on the plan to redesign the process and instead merely make marginal improvements in components of the current system. I'm sure that the committee's view that an ROC analysis of accuracy was appropriate was threatening to SSA representatives, with me there to urge that it be done correctly. This outcome meant that the IOM committee would function as a consultant to the SSA on an ad hoc basis—a relationship NRC or IOM committees are supposed to avoid. I felt strongly enough about that to resign from the committee, and did so. I had a conversation with Kenneth Shine, the president of the IOM and a friend, who had gotten me involved with the two IOM committees, about why it hadn't turned out so well.

I had consulted earlier and briefly on disability policies for a Florida-based legal organization and noted that the process of disability determination has a decision-threshold problem as well as an accuracy problem. Specifically, in the present system the threshold changes dramatically from the initial level of a claim evaluation to an appeals level. Roughly two-thirds of cases first denied and then appealed are allowed at the second level; award rates at the appeals level are more than twice those at the initial level. A class-action suit by the legal association was brought to remedy the plight of initially denied applicants who are not aware of the potential of making a formal appeal. Application of a feature-analysis approach as discussed in chapter 6 would give a "disability score" and then a threshold could be consistently set on that numerical continuum.

Board on Behavioral, Cognitive, and Sensory Sciences

During my final year as CBASSE chair, I worked with staff to set up a new board called the Board on Behavioral, Cognitive, and Sensory Sciences (BBCS). It was intended in part to give the developing cognitive sciences a formal place in CBASSE and to promote a cause I had been working on: the application of cognitive sciences to learning and education. I had, for example, held a meeting at BBN of cognitive scientists, including Ann Brown, Allan Collins, J. C. Campione, and Sandy Wigdor, to garner ideas about the most ready applications. Several NRC studies followed, one of the earliest and most prominent being reported in "How People Learn," edited by J. D. Bransford, A. L. Brown, and R. Cocking.

Some of us also felt that it was time to relate the long-standing vision and hearing committees to other CBASSE sciences and they were folded into this new board. The chairs of those committees at the time, Bill Yost and Peter Lennie, joined the board constructively, to help ease the pain for sensory scientists. I served on this board for three years, my last association with the NRC.

Coda

My associations with the NAS and NRC have been highlights among my memories, professionally and personally. I think of many gatherings at the Washington, D.C., Irvine, and Woods Hole campuses, including the garden parties.

8   Five Easy Pieces

Invitations came to me in early retirement to write five particular articles. By coincidence, as a group, they summarize very well both my career and the career of detection theory. Respectively, these articles treat graduate school at Michigan, history of signal detection theory, early years at BBN, and (two of them) general diagnostic science and diagnostic decisions in several applied fields. Here, the articles are cited and abstracted, and excerpted to the extent that they round out this story.

Graduate School

"Alumni Spotlight: John Swets AB'50, AM'53, PhD'54," *On Our Minds, Annual Newsletter,* University of Michigan Department of Psychology, Summer 2006, Issue 8, p. 44

In response to a one-question "interview," I reflect in this newsletter on how work done throughout my career was based on explorations begun at the University of Michigan, as covered in chapter 3 of this memoir.

History of SDT

"Sensation and Perception: Signal Detection Theory, History," *Encyclopedia of the Social and Behavioral Sciences,* Elsevier Science Ltd. 2001

An encyclopedia entry presents the story of SDT across its spectrum—

in statistical theory, communications engineering, psychology, and diagnostics—and from its inception to the present.

The theory of testing statistical hypotheses (or statistical inference) was generalized in the theory of statistical decision-making and contributed almost all that was needed for modern signal detection theory. Peterson and Birdsall devised the "receiver operating characteristic" (ROC) to show, in a simple graph, how detection theory provides independent measures of the detection accuracy and the decision threshold of a receiver (observer). In a word, the curve is a plot of the proportion of true positives against the proportion of false positives; the curve's locus in the square (say, the percentage of area beneath it) conveys the degree of accuracy while points along the curve reflect the possible decision thresholds (as measured, for example, by the slope of the curve at a given point).

In the ROC's move from engineering to psychology, Jim Egan and I separately showed how it could be produced empirically in a single observing session (with a single group of observations), by the so-called *confidence-rating* method, rather than in the half-dozen or so sessions required by the *yes-no* method (each with a different threshold). With the rating method, the observer would rate each observation on, say, a five- or ten- or hundred-point scale as to its likelihood of representing a signal's presence. The rating method can define an ROC with about 200 observations as compared to the approximate 1,200 observations (200 per point) needed by the yes-no method—and gives the observer a simpler task. Jim and I validated the rating method by showing that it gave essentially the same results as the yes-no method. Actually, the rating method gives less variable measures, probably because it is obtained in a shorter time, under more constant conditions. As described in the article:

> Validating the rating method ... had the important effect of providing an efficient method for obtaining empirical ROCs. Whereas under the yes-no method the observer is induced to set a different cutpoint [threshold] in each of several observing sessions (each providing a single ROC point), under the rating method the observer effectively maintains several decision cutpoints simultaneously (the boundaries of the rating categories) so that several empirical ROC cutpoints (enough to define a curve) can be obtained in one observing session.

The analysis made by the rating method can be applied to any situation in which "scores" along a continuum give the relative likelihood that a "signal" is present—not necessarily scores assigned by an observer. For example, an information- retrieval system may assign a score to each item in the collection giving its relevance to the query at hand.

Again, a blood test may assign a range of values of PSA, with successively higher values giving greater likelihoods of prostate cancer.

The new-found efficiency made subsequent applications of SDT practical—both in psychology and diagnostics. It was clearly the difference between extensive use and little use of the ROC. ROC use was further facilitated when Don Dorfman and Charles Metz—first independently and then jointly—developed software to fit ROC curves to continuous, "rating" data and made it freely available. Similar programs became part of the various commercial software packages available.

Flash back to some of the thinking underlying the possible application of SDT to sensory processes in psychology, as set forth in this encyclopedia article:

> In 1952, Tanner and Swets joined Peterson and Birdsall as staff in a laboratory of the electrical engineering department called the Electronic Defense Group. They were aware of then-new conceptions of neural functioning in which stimulus inputs found an already active nervous system and neurons were not lying quiescent till fired at full force. In short, neural noise as well as environmental noise was likely to be a factor in detection and then the observer's task is readily conceived as a choice between statistical hypotheses [noise alone or signal-plus-noise]. Though a minority idea in the history of psychophysics, the possibility that the observer deliberately sets a cutpoint on a continuous variable (weight of evidence) seemed likely to Tanner and Swets. A budding cognitive psychology (e.g., "new look" in perception) supported the notion of extrasensory determinants of perceptual phenomena, as represented in SDT by expectancies (prior probabilities) and motivation (benefits and costs).

Psychology at BBN

"The ABC's of BBN: From Acoustics to Behavioral Sciences to Computers," *IEEE Annals of the History of Computing,* 22(2), April-June 2005, pp. 15–29

In a two-volume set of articles devoted to BBN's early history, Leo Beranek opened with "BBN's Earliest Days; Founding a Culture of Engineering Creativity," and my article followed.

As did several historians, I noted the influence of psychology on computers and traced a path from Harvard University to MIT to BBN. Psychology and acoustics were joined at Harvard and then at MIT and then at BBN, when Beranek and Licklider moved along that path. Lick followed Leo to BBN in order to work on computers as well as psychoacoustics there. Information processing and man-machine interaction were his interests, along with auditory theory and speech communication. While at MIT, he spent time at Lincoln Laboratory, working with the computers that led to the PDP-1, which was later to arrive at BBN in its prototype form, for testing, and then as the first production model. This machine was a large departure from the computers of the day and BBN went on to develop time-sharing of a single computer among several on-line users; to engineer, build, and manage the first computer network (the ARPANET); and to make the innovation of person-to-person e-mail. (Ray Tomlinson wrote the e-mail software on his own over a weekend.) Lick's ideas organized computer research and development at BBN from the 1950s through the present, as carried out by some 500 computer and psychologist scientists and engineers.[1]

The Science of Diagnosis

"Psychological Science Can Improve Diagnostic Decisions," (coauthored with R. M. Dawes and J. Monahan), *Psychological Science in the Public Interest.* A journal of the American Psychological Society (APS) (now Association for Psychological Science) 1(1), May 2000, pp. 1–26

The APS inaugurated the journal *PSPI* in 2000 to "give psychology away." Each issue addresses a topic of public interest in an area where psychological science has the potential to inform and improve public policy. Each issue represents the efforts of a distinguished team of scientists to report the available evidence, and the implications of that evidence, fairly and comprehensively—a juried analysis. Stephen Ceci and Robert Bjork were coeditors, the idea of the journal having sprung from their agile minds; I was a member of the editorial board.

Bob Bjork somehow convinced me and the board that I should form a team to prepare the first issue, on the topic of diagnostic science. With the editors' encouragement, I recruited my top choices, Robin Dawes and John Monahan. We went to work promptly and published our report a year earlier than scheduled. Our report made the point that many diagnoses are distinctions between two alternatives and are reflected in a binary (for example, yes-no) judgment, citing as examples "Is a cancer present?" "Will this individual commit violence?" "Are there explosives

---

1. BBN's commercial network-communications business, TELNET, was sold to GTE and later became SPRINT. The entirety of BBN was acquired by GTE in 1997. GTE, including BBN, was acquired by Bell Atlantic in 2000, to form Verizon. The core business of BBN—the laboratories—was separated from Verizon to go back on its own in 2003, through a sale to venture capitalists. As this book goes to press in the fall of 2009, BBN Technologies is in the process of being acquired by the Raytheon company.

in this luggage?" "Will the stock market advance today?" "Is this assembly-line item flawed?" "Is this aircraft fit to fly?" "Will an impending storm strike?" "Is there oil in the ground here?" "Is there an unsafe radiation level in my house?" "Is this person lying?" "Is this person using drugs?" "Will this applicant succeed?" "Is this applicant legally disabled?" "Is that plane intending to attack this ship?" "Will this book have the information I need?" "Does this tax return justify an audit?"

The report, as the reader will suspect, presents the ways in which signal detection theory and related statistical analyses can serve to evaluate and enhance diagnostic accuracy and illustrates the manner in which an appropriate decision threshold may be selected. To relieve the *Sturm und Drang* of many of our previous applications (crashes and tumors), we made a small foray into aesthetics. One application discussed was the correlation between subjective sound quality in twenty-three opera houses, as rated by twenty-two conductors, and the combination of acoustical variables ('features' in our terms) measured physically in those opera houses (data collected by Leo Beranek). Designers can use those data to enhance sound quality. A second application was the prediction of the quality of a vintage of mature wine (market price at auction) from measurements of climatic variables during the growing season, a prediction that can be made accurately when the wine is young and undrinkable, and therefore when the usual clinical, tasting method is unreliable.

I wrote a guest column in the APS newsletter (the *Observer)* describing my experiences in preparation of the report, entitled "I was the *PSPI* Canary." I revealed that APS had sent me down into a mine and I had come up with a song. I wanted to encourage APS members to be involved in the process—as authors, reviewers, consultants, researchers who propose topics, and individuals who bring the *PSPI* reports to others who can use the information.

"Better Decisions through Science" (coauthored with R. M. Dawes and J. Monahan), *Scientific American,* 283, October 2000, pp. 82–87

PSPI's board and the APS leadership advanced the cause of the new journal appreciably by arranging a partnership with the magazine *Scientific American.* John Rennie, editor-in-chief, worked with *PSPI editors* and APS officials to develop a collaboration in which *PSPI* reports are rewritten for *Scientific American*'s broad audience. Rennie's editorial to accompany the first *PSPI*-based article describes his hopes for the collaboration, as follows:

SMART CHOICES

Decisions, decisions. We all make them every day, and thank heaven mine are always right, but can you imagine the anxiety felt by those people with flawed judgment?

Take the stressful lives of diagnosticians in medicine and industry, whose choices tip the balance between life and death. In their perfect world, diagnoses would be easy because the evidence would unambiguously and without fail point to the true underlying condition. In their slightly less perfect world, knowledge of the occasional misdiagnoses would be tempered by certainty that they had caused a minimum of damage. But our world is the planet Earth, where the motto is "Not for the Squeamish."

And yet there is hope. As the authors of "Better Decisions through Science" convincingly argue, beginning on page 82, statistical aids can often improve diagnoses. Moreover, this mathematical approach—don't worry, it's fairly simple—works even with decisions that have traditionally been seen as qualitative and subjective, such as parole assessments of violent felons. I strongly recommend this article to politicians, managers, physicians, educators, and anyone else routinely making tough choices; it will make you think.

This article inaugurates a series of collaborations ... Leadership in the APS recognized that the public's awareness of psychological research is poor. The best and most reliable findings are lost in the haze of headline-grabbing reports that often make conflicting or spurious claims. *PSPI* will therefore publish "white papers" summarizing the conclusions of a jury of experts that has weighed the published evidence on topics of national concern. Future issues may consider such matters as: Do smaller class sizes improve students' academic achievement? Is controlled drinking a safe alternative to abstinence for alcoholics? Can ginkgo and other herbal products enhance cognitive function?

To help disseminate these findings as widely as possible, *Scientific American* is working with the authors of the *PSPI* scholarly papers to publish versions aimed more at the general public. Our hope is that these articles will inform political and social discussions to good effect.

Hopes are generously satisfied. Executive Director of APS Alan Kraut confirms currently that *PSPI* has flourished, for example, increasing from two to four issues a year. The *PSPI-Scientific American* collaboration is going strong, both with the regular magazine and with the newer magazine, *Scientific American Mind*. In addition, *PSPI* is getting excellent press coverage broadly—in *The New York Times,* the *Wall Street Journal, USA Today, Newsweek,* and so on.

Tributes to the Work

The 1994 White House policy report *Science in the National Interest* (listed authors: William J. Clinton and Albert Gore, Jr.) selected this body of SDT applications to illustrate the importance of basic behavioral science research. The report's summary of the work concluded: "Thus, the methods of behavioral science go hand in hand with the physical and biological sciences." and "... the technique promises improved ... public health and safety."

Another assessment of SDT applications comes from one of psychology's elder statesmen, William K. Estes: "Over ensuing decades, the SD[T] model, with only technical modifications to accommodate particular applications, has become almost universally accepted as a theoretical account of decision making in research on perceptual detection and recognition and in numerous extensions to applied domains (Swets, 1988; Swets, Dawes, and Monahan, 2000). This development may well be regarded as the most towering achievement of basic psychological research of the last half century." I can settle for that.

9   Family, Fun, and Games

T his concluding chapter is a pastiche. I touch on some doings away
from the office, usually with the family, often recreational.

Travel

Elder son Steve accompanied me to Moscow in 1966 when he was fifteen and had a grand time. He found another American his age (Neal
Miller's son) and they had the run of the city for a week. When a group
of conference goers, abandoned by their bus, got lost after a Volga boat
trip, he led us back to our hotel, having become acquainted with the
subway system.

Steve and I stopped for a few days on the way over in Copenhagen
and Stockholm and, on our return, at the Villa d' Este on Lake Como,
where he signed up for a job as pool attendant for the next summer. He
was able to take a friend with him.[1] The pool manager, Tony Botta, was
a university student who visited us in Lexington the next year, and hired
younger son Joe for a pool job the following year.

Steve and I also stopped in Paris. He had taken French for a few years

---

1. I visited Steve and his friend Nat at the Villa d' Este and took them to dinner at the
hotel. Unforgettably, they indulged the specific hunger for fresh orange juice that they
had built up at staff meals, each of them going through a half-dozen tall glasses at a cost
I've suppressed.

and told friends back home that my French was restricted to "ici garçon," pronounced "icky garkon." At Como, Steve rode his moped a few times to Switzerland; Joe managed to fit in a weekend in Rome. They both spent their summer's pay on Rolex watches.

The Russians were great fans of signal detection theory. I have nine books sent to me by Russian scientists with extensive treatments of the theory. At the Moscow meeting, I was invited by several of them to laboratories in Leningrad, but travel arrangements were so tenuous that I didn't have the nerve to go. For example, Moscow hotel staff took our passports and threw them into a large box—so that retrieving them on departure took awhile, when we were under time pressure. We felt under strain in Moscow, because of difficulties getting meals, taxis, phone calls, and so forth, some of which seemed to arise out of malice. Just how much strain there was, was indicated by an impulsive sigh that swept the cabin of our return flight when the captain announced that we were flying over the Russian border into Austria. We traveled with the Neal Miller family without Neal who had been held unaccountably at the Moscow airport; he joined his family two days later in Vienna. In response to specific hungers built up in Moscow, upon arriving in Vienna I ordered chocolate cake, Coca Cola, and a fried egg, in that sequence.

Dave Green and I met French psychologist Anne-Marie Bonnel, who was interested in detection theory, at a Paris meeting. Dave and I drove along the Rhone and visited Anne-Marie and her husband François at their home near Aix-en-Provence, which gave a view of Picasso's castle and Cezanne's mountain from poolside. The Bonnels showed us Provence's wonders (Les Baux, Camargue, and so on) and later visited us at our homes in Winchester, Massachusetts.

Edinburgh is a favorite city. I went back under various excuses and played "golf in the kingdom." Bob Bjork, son Joe, and I made a tour of a half-dozen Scottish golf courses, high-lighted by two rounds at St. Andrews. Joe and I stayed a night near Prestwick with our friends the Cassels. Another year, Joe visited the Bjorks in St. Andrews, when they spent the summer at the university. After a meeting of the International Society for Psychophysics in Stirling, Scotland, a part of the group biked and hiked across the country; I joined the concluding hike across the rugged Rannoch Moor.

Bob Bjork and I took our golf games to several attractive spots. I'll ask him if this list is near complete: Central, Southeastern, and Winchester,

Massachusetts (with Dan Schacter); Cape Cod; Hanover, New Hampshire; Tequesta, Jupiter, and Tampa, Florida; and a few courses near his home in the Los Angeles area. Bob's wife Elizabeth joined us occasionally. Dave Green and I enjoyed (pro-tour favorite) Torrey Pines in La Jolla several times while he was on the faculty at the University of California, San Diego.

I traveled twice to Berlin, the first time in 1979 to attend a workshop on medical imaging in West Berlin sponsored by the Dahlem Konferenzen. The Dahlem interdisciplinary conferences follow a set structure of background papers, plenary and small group discussions, and rapporteur sessions, and produce a book at the end of the week. I visited the Dahlem museum, where I acquired prints I still enjoy. For example, Brueghel's depiction of thirty or so German proverbs (the hectic scene reminded one of my colleagues of a typical day at BBN).

The conference group took a side trip to East Berlin, via Checkpoint Charlie, where I had arranged to meet H.-G. Geissler during a stop at Humboldt University; I was to help him arrange an international conference on psychophysics. That the KGB had taken notice of this little meeting became evident when they stopped a Dahlem conference attendee who had gone into East Berlin on his own and accused him of being me. That eerie event discouraged me from attending a conference in Leipzig a few years later (for which the travel was going to be difficult anyhow).

I made a second trip to Berlin to attend a meeting of the board of the German-American Research Foundation, after the fall of The Wall, in East Berlin. The visits to the Pergamon and Bauhaus museums and Potsdam were fun, but the "highlight" of the week was the occurrence of the annual European "Love In," attended by thousands. I don't think I can begin to describe this bacchanalia, or that you would want me to.

Details of other trips are hazy, but I recall a boat trip down the Rhine from Cologne to Salzburg, a train trip from Cassis, France, to St. Vincent, Italy, a conference dinner in a castle at Kungalv, Sweden, and stays at university and travelers' clubs on Pall Mall in London. In two days at the Rijksmuseum in Amsterdam, I acquired several prints, for example, a grouping of a Rembrandt self portrait, his portraits of his mother and son, and "The Nightwatch." Son Joe and I once arranged a trip to the Middle East, but canceled when a hundred or so tourists were blown up in Cairo, our planned first stop. I never made it east of Moscow nor west of Los Angeles, which seemed too far for a skittish flyer.

Moves

For the record, we lived in Ann Arbor at 123 Fairview Avenue, in Lexington at 8 Blueberry Lane and 111 Kendall Road, and in Winchester at 35 Myopia Hill Road. In Tequesta, Florida, we began vacationing at Riverbend in 1978 and later at North Passage, in condominiums we owned, and in 2002 we moved in the same neighborhood to Turtle Creek East, on the Loxahatchee River. This is Southeast Florida. Our initial forays to this area were occasioned by my parents living in Lake Worth, just south of Palm Beach.

Country Clubs

Mickey and I serially joined three country/golf clubs. The Lexington Golf Club, strictly golf, nine holes, in 1965. We may have thought of it as a present for our surviving a dental accident. A whirling sanding disc came off the drilling tool and cut up the inside of my mouth, after which an oral surgeon sewed it up tightly enough that it couldn't drain and it swelled a lot. Mickey took me to a hospital where they immediately performed a tracheotomy. We had another present waiting for me when I came home: a new television set capable of receiving the channel that would show the NCAA Final Four basketball game that night between Princeton (Bill Bradley) and Michigan (Cazzie Russell).

Parenthesis. The dental accident led to another hospital visit a few years later for follow-up surgery. In those days of yore, I checked into the Phillips House of the Massachusetts General Hospital the evening before, and had a nice chat with my anesthesiologist. She came to my room afterward and asked if I remembered our recovery-room conversation. No. She said that she had told me that I could go back to my room and read a psychology book, and I had replied: " I don't *read* 'em, Sister, I *write* 'em." You can think of the truth serum as revealing my true arrogant self or, better, of me (or her) as making a little joke.

I played most of the golf at Lexington, re Mickey, and was pleasantly successful, winning a club handicap championship and two two-man team championships.

We joined the Winchester Country Club in 1972 when we moved from Lexington to Winchester. Mickey became a competitive golfer and she and a friend won a woman's member-member championship. She and I won a mixed, handicap championship, by qualifying for the championship flight and then winning eighteen-hole matches on three successive weekends. I won a super-seniors handicap championship under the same format (one week after becoming eligible).

We joined the Tequesta Country Club when we moved to Tequesta in 1998. Just one championship so far: a men's member-member. Come on down and I'll show you the gilt calligraphy on a mahogany plaque. The club is reachable from our condominium by golf cart and maintains a fine dining room. Tomorrow is an Easter brunch.

Curling

We took up curling when we moved to Winchester, an absolutely wonderful game. Casual visitors compare watching curling to watching grass grow, but one has to experience the thrill of laying the final rock, after two hours of play and stratagems, when the game depends on it. Decisions to factor in include: whether to go for an overtime or a win, how heavy (fast) to lay the rock, how much curl to give it, what line, how much sweeping to figure on, which opponent rocks to knock out, and so forth.

Mickey and I curled two to three times a week all winter, home and away—in men's, women's, and mixed events. I stayed in the Boston area, where there were four other curling venues, but she traveled farther afield. Many trips to The Country Club in Brookline were a special treat. We won a few club championships as the "front end," that is, the less competent, junior members of the four-person team. Notably, we won one club championship that we "skipped"—that is, called the shots and played last in each end (inning). Curlers exchange handsome club pins at bonspiels and we have a bunch from Canadian rinks (teams) and from New York and the Midwest.

Our other winter sport was cross-country skiing, which we would do in New Hampshire (say, Bretton Woods) or on the golf course in Winchester that we could ski to. I was introduced to the sport at the first of George Sperling's Annual Interdisciplinary Conferences, at Jackson Hole, Wyoming.

Bridge

Bridge is Mickey's game—she has the knack and then some. She directed the faculty-wives play at the University of Michigan and at MIT. I played socially—with no discipline—over the years but am now gaining respect for the game. Learning new conventions for more precise bidding can be fun. We play mostly in regular men's and women's groups at the local country club.[2]

Club Acoustics

My acquaintance with the architectural acoustics activity at BBN led to improvements at three clubs. Winchester Country Club found the acoustics deplorable after renovations of two dining rooms; BBN's Parker Hirtle fixed that with the appropriate ceiling tiles.

Son Steve's father-in-law was a member of the Nantucket Yacht Club when it decided to panel with handsome hardwood every surface in the dining room, including the ceilings; the windows had to be opened to permit people standing side-by-side to understand each other. BBN's Jack Curtis drew the trip to the Island and convinced the club management to replace the wood on the ceiling with something softer.

For the Tequesta Country Club, a BBN friend directed me to an acoustic consultant in Miami who could fix a large, new dining room. This consultant won the club's gratitude by not suggesting that drapes be hung at the floor-to-ceiling windows running 270 degrees around the room. The vaulted ceiling could not be directly resurfaced, having more than one hundred recessed speakers and flood lights, and no crawl space to permit dropping them, so the consultant made many measurements to guide the hanging of special, two-inch-thick panels of different sizes (up to two feet by five feet) across the room, at different distances from the ceiling (from two to six inches). All that science worked just fine. But now I have to remind a new board of directors how the panels got there; I hear they are planning to take them down, as part of a renovation, or perhaps to paint them.

Architects don't stress enough the importance of adequate acoustic treatment during design, because everyone is seeking to cut costs, it's not pretty, and the good it does is difficult for the client to anticipate. BBN's Leo Beranek learned this again painfully and publicly when (in 1962) he attempted to design—under severe restrictions—the acoustics

---

2. I watch sports on television to an extent that I can't ignore here: University of Michigan football and basketball and three "local" teams, namely, Boston Celtics, New England Patriots, and Miami Dolphins. (It's a plus that the two professional football teams have Michigan quarterbacks now.) Then there are Boston College for Michael and the University of Miami for Caroline. Professional golfers get a look in the major tournaments. The Boston Red Sox get a look when they reach the World Series.

of the Lincoln Center's new Philharmonic Hall; initial reactions of conductors and critics were negative and the hall was then retrofitted.

"The Boys"

Sons Steve and Joe are in their fifties, both living in Massachusetts—in the towns of Westborough and Winchester, respectively. Steve met his wife, Diana Murray, when they were students at Lawrence University in Wisconsin; Joe is single.

Steve's and Di's children are Michael and Caroline. Mike graduated from Boston College and Caroline from Westborough High in 2009—both with honors. Mike wants to coach Division 1 basketball, and was chosen from among a host of applicants (I believe there were 190) for a position on the coaching staff at Providence College (where he will also pursue a two-year masters degree). Caroline is pointing toward a degree in nursing at the University of Miami (as I write this, her parents are in Miami today for homecoming). They'll both continue to make their grandparents proud.

As I write this paragraph, the extended Swets and Murray families look forward to next weekend's NCAA Final Four basketball event. About twelve of us have made our picks, supported by a five-dollar entry fee. Steve is in the lead; he told me today that I couldn't win no matter what happens the rest of the way.

Steve is working in advertising again after a long stint with Fidelity Investments in Boston, for awhile as a vice president. His connection with Fidelity began in his early twenties, while in an earlier position in advertising. On his first day in that job, the agency gave him the Fidelity account to manage—a new client just beginning to advertise. We say that Fidelity and Steve grew up together. Diana teaches French and Spanish at Westborough Middle School—and, like my mother, has logged significant time teaching her children. The Spanish should stand Caroline in good stead at the University of Miami and during a month in Spain this summer.

Joe is a graduate of Colby College, where, during his freshman year, he and many other fraternity members were put on Dean's Office probation following the fraternity's excessive St. Patrick's Day celebration. A few weeks later he was appointed to the Student Judicial Board, which he later chaired. (Joe had always been a good one-trial learner, no pun intended.)

Joe went on to earn a J.D. from Suffolk University Law School, where he later was a part-time adjunct professor. He also holds a masters degree in taxation from Boston University School of Law and held a federal court clerkship in Washington, D.C. Now, after practicing law in Boston for almost twenty years, Joe has retired from that field. Since 2006 he has been executive director of Cummings Foundation—a private operating foundation on the way to becoming a grant-making foundation.

Both boys attended kindergarten through high school in Lexington. They were nonplussed when their empty-nest parents then moved to an adjacent town, arch-rival Winchester. They had competed in track and cross-country. Steve went on to participate in track at Lawrence University, in what I consider to be the grittiest of the sport's events, the 440-yard high hurdles. I roomed with Big Ten 440 champ Herb Barton and gained respect for the distance; now Steve was doing that distance with high obstacles strewn in his path! He captained the team in his final year.

Both Steve and Joe were exposed to signal detection theory in college, Joe in an introductory psychology course and an upper-level course on vision. Steve's introductory professor remarked to the class on the first day that they would be studying psychological ideas that Steve's father had developed—and also singled out a young woman as the grandniece (I believe) of Gestalt psychologist Wolfgang Kohler.

When young, say, nine to twelve, they could both beat me handily at chess. "Handily" meaning that that each would bring a comic book to the table to keep himself amused while I planned my next move. When I made it, my opponent would swoop in and make his move and return to the book. On first thought, I was astounded. On second thought, I sort of understood it. On third thought, there is something profound here that I don't get. Is learning chess like learning a spoken language, best when one is young? Learning to play the piano must be a snap after years of computer games: see a symbol, make the corresponding keystroke. (We calibrated the boy's chess games favorably against that of Rocco Urbano, a mathematician friend who seemed quite knowledgeable about the game.)

Diana Murray grew up on Nantucket Island. She is daughter of Philip and Elizabeth, who have owned and operated Murray's Toggery, the busy shop at the head of Main Street—the one that purveys faded red slacks, and whales on belts and ties. The Island has been a wonderful place for Di's and Steve's family to visit often—and the same for Mickey and me; we have visited less frequently, but often, and have many times been the beneficiaries of Phil's and Elizabeth's hospitality. Mickey and I have also enjoyed being guests of Chet and Mary Baker when Chet and I played in the annual member-guest golf tournament at the Sankaty Head Golf Club. These wonderful visits began with Di's and Steve's wedding on the island, a long weekend enjoyed by several of our off-island friends.[3]

New England Vacations

As long as our family was vacationing together, we typically spent July at Lake Sunapee or Lake Winnipesaukee, in New Hampshire, and a few times at smaller lakes in New Hampshire and Maine. Each time, we had use of a small powerboat to take us into town. At Lake Sunapee, we shared a cottage with the Houghtons, with their two daughters, or stayed near the Matthews. We had friends near Wolfeboro on Winnipesaukee. For awhile, we were members of the Bald Peak Club there. Some summers were social, but most were as low key as we could make them.

Later, several long weekends were enjoyed with Nancy and Gus Wunder in their second home at Eastman, New Hampshire, a recreational community halfway between Lake Sunapee and Hanover. Mickey and I first met the Wunders when they and we moved to Winchester in 1972, they after several years in Wimbledon and London, and we became fast friends. We have golfed, curled, skied cross-country, exchanged books and movies, spent holidays, and played bridge together. Gus and I have spent happy, competitive hours at his pool table (where my mis-spent youth is hard to deny); I can't touch him at backgammon. They now have a second home a block away from our condominium in Tequesta.[4]

---

3. Bill Gates plays golf on Nantucket Island, and today's paper indicates that "his people" are looking for real estate on Jupiter Island, adjacent to our town, Tequesta. Our residences being in the same zip code won't mean that our properties are equally valued.

4. We have been able to keep abreast of other long-time friends since our move to Florida, thanks to visits (one to several) by the Bjorks, Birneys, Pews, King-Naceys, Carlsons, and Connellys. We have stayed in touch with still other friends, too numerous to list, through e-mails, telephone calls, and holiday cards.

Half an Oaf?

Calvin Trillin, in an article In the opinion pages of yesterday's newspaper ("Half an Oaf," *The New York Times,* April 12, 2009), wondered, as he said his family does, whether or not he is an *uncultured oaf.* He adduces his difficulty with the few subtitled movies he saw long ago and his enjoying a modern-dance program, choreographed by a friend, without being aware that it had a plot. He mentions growing up in the Midwest—"in a milieu in which culture did not hang heavily in the air. As was customary in that time and place, my mother took my sister to concerts and road shows of Broadway musicals while my father took me to the Golden Gloves and the N.C.A.A. Basketball tournaments. (We all went to the American Royal Livestock Show together.)"

As a midwesterner like Trillin, I have to be interested in his question. What comes to mind is my parents taking my sister and me to hear the singing Russian Cossacks, and my fascination as a sixth grader with the senior-class play, *The Moonstone.* (To an extent we overcame: for one, Mickey and I did pretty well by the theater during our years in Boston.) To extend this introspection, I wonder if Trillin asks himself whether or not he is an *intellectual.* (I suppose he feels that he is, by definition, if he writes Op-Ed articles.) As I near the end of this memoir, I note that the organizing and writing process has sharpened for me my sense of identity, reflecting as I have on where I came from, what I have been, who I am, what I have accomplished and not accomplished. I will never have more information to consider regarding these two questions than I have right now; I am compelled to say that the evidence is mixed.

Performing Before Groups

I wrote a cryptic sentence in the second paragraph of the first chapter of this volume that may be clarified now. Although my mother, dad, and I noticed a quality of shyness in each other, we actually enjoyed performing, in our respective ways, before audiences, say, of thirty to one-hundred people. Mom presented programs of her design and research on biblical subjects to women's church groups. For example, she would tell an interesting story of "The Apostles," accompanied by handsome portraits, and interspersed with vocal solos by young friends of hers. She did so over a span of eight to ten years, I estimate, to a few dozen groups.

Dad spoke before, or more often chaired, meetings of various school and civic groups. Perhaps "toastmaster" was the operative term. I extrapolate now from the few such meetings that I attended—to, I imagine, most of them. As if he couldn't help himself, he would keep the group laughing throughout the session—without a single joke he had heard elsewhere, with entirely spontaneous topical remarks—making sure meanwhile to cover the agenda to be covered.

I caught the trait from my dad and carried it spontaneously to a disparate set of groups: a golf championship banquet, a national professional society, a church meeting while I served as church moderator, and several less organized assemblies. I remember them vividly for the sheer fun. (Of course, I would turn off the humor switch when making a scientific address, when every single minute was needed to communicate.)

Retirement Party

BBN was so good as to let me stay on the staff until I was seventy, although for the final five years it retired half of my salary. Actually, I kept an office and secretarial assistance for two years beyond seventy. At the retirement party, my family and I heard nice things said about them and me by Jim Barger, Dick Pew, John Makhoul, and Shelly Baron. I was given a piece of Steuben crystal (which joined a ship's clock I had received after twenty-five years on the staff). The company's senior managers at the time were professional managers who had the crystal's base inscribed "for 36 years of dedicated service;" they hadn't picked up on the company's culture, to make the inscription read "for 36 years of valuable contributions." They compensated nicely by taking us to a cordial dinner at one of Boston's finest restaurants, where sons Steve and Joe made some kind remarks about their old man.

Afterword

To have the opportunity to organize my personal and professional memories in print in my ninth decade is to be blessed with multiple gifts. There is the fulfillment that comes from creating a personal and partial family history for my children's and grandchildren's generations. I additionally found it fulfilling to "arrange" my story and the story of my life's work in psychophysics in a way that interested me and, I hope, will interest some close professional colleagues and personal friends. If a few other scientists with whom I had no or only a passing acquaintance are interested in this framing of the ROC story and its provenance, then so much the better.

This little book is a valentine to the family that nurtured me (including uncles, aunts, and cousins) and the family that Mickey and I started and nurtured in turn, and to a working life spent in psychological science.

My contemporaries should relate to a childhood influenced by the Great Depression. I was fortunate to have parents and extended family that by dint of hard work, strong wills, and love of family and community, saw to it that my sister and I were well cared for and guided down productive paths in our formative years. Mickey and I were also quite fortunate to find each other as Midwestern teens (though some say I might have been luckier than she); we are the proud parents of two sons and a daughter-in-law, and have two grandchildren as grand as all others. We celebrated our sixtieth anniversary earlier this year.

In my career, I was pretty nearly always in the right place at the right time. Early on, I fell in with a core group of friends and mentors in the Michigan psychology department where collegial cooperation resulted in early successes for the group, and got each of us off to career head starts. I studied "dust bowl" psychophysics and helped make the field exciting by a role in converting it to a "cognitive" enterprise. Peterson, Birdsall, and Tanner were there when I needed them.

Eventually, signal detection theory impacted a wide range of psychological and other studies, essentially any that involve fine discriminations. I was fortunate to be at the forefront in adapting SDT and ROC techniques to varied areas of diagnosis; I believe it fair to say now that the theory and technique offer a partial but substantial *science of diagnosis*. I was privileged to meet large numbers of scientists and become conversant with many scientific problems in several disciplines. BBN was there for me, allowing me to do as I wished. I had the opportunity to interpret SDT and the ROC in journals over the years as they developed; *Science* magazine was particularly generous with its space.

As I reflect on my life in science, with the fabled twenty-twenty vision of hindsight, I am grateful for the career I was afforded amidst developing scientific disciplines and vibrant organizations. Early challenges declined and relationships became consistently congenial. There was surely room to do better professionally, but all in all, I won't be asking for a 'do-over.'

Acknowledgments

Son Stephen suggested that I write a personal history, gave me encouragement along the way, assured me that grandson Michael and granddaughter Caroline would be interested, suggested photographs for the book, and offered to prepare them for printing. Son Joel commented on the manuscript as it grew, suggesting possible additions and deletions. I was glad when my topics and prose met with his approval and grateful for his care packages containing chapters with marginal notations. Wife Mickey tried her best to get me to dispense with the small stuff and detail in the early chapters; as to the rest, she gave me more reinforcement than I could have hoped for. Rod Jellema, childhood friend among the tulips, sharpened my recollections of Holland. A professor of English, he refrained mostly from commenting on my writing; what evaluation I did extract from between the lines was reassuring to me. Richard Pew read the manuscript line-by-line and offered a page or two of comments, editorial and technical, on each major chapter. He knew whereof he spoke, having been affiliated with the principal institutions: Michigan psychology, BBN, Harvard psychology, and the National Research Council. (Disclosure: he and I shared an office at BBN when I arrived.) Marilyn Adams, researcher and author at BBN, showed once more that she knows how to mix steady approval and sufficient praise with novel ideas. Robert Birney, fellow graduate student, after seeing the first three chapters convinced me that the book needed an organizing principle and then gave me one. I didn't use it as well as I should have, but managed to show some parallels and interactions between a theory's career and mine. Robert Earl, another Michigan student, reinforced me generously as sets of draft chapters reached him. Charles Metz offered to announce the publication of this book on his popular website for ROC software. David Walden introduced me to many of the wonders of publishing in the digital age. Charles Wiseman of Peninsula Publishing, who has reprinted two of my books since 1988, took publication of this memoir under his wing and I am pleased to see it among the fine works of his firm.

LaVergne, TN USA
30 April 2010
181126LV00004B/39/P